THE POLITICAL LIVES OF DEAD BODIES

THE HARRIMAN LECTURES

THE HARRIMAN LECTURES

Thanks to the generosity and foresight of the W. Averell Harriman family, the annual Harriman Lectures have become an important intellectual event and celebration in the academic calendar of the Institute and Columbia University. Previous Harriman Lectures have been delivered by the noted American social scientist Barrington Moore, the Russian academician and cultural historian Dmitri Likhachev, the late British economist Alec Nove, and the late British social theorist Ernest Gellner. In 1996 the lectures were increased from one to three, and a program of publication commenced with Columbia University Press.

ALREADY PUBLISHED

—Andrei Sinyavsky, *The Russian Intelligentsia*, 1997

THE POLITICAL LIVES
OF DEAD BODIES
Reburial and Postsocialist Change

Katherine Verdery

COLUMBIA UNIVERSITY PRESS   NEW YORK

COLUMBIA UNIVERSITY PRESS

Publishers Since 1893

New York   Chichester, West Sussex

Library of Congress Cataloging-in-Publication Data

Verdery, Katherine.

The political lives of dead bodies : reburial and postsocialist change / Katherine Verdery.

  p. cm. — (The Harriman Lectures)

  Includes bibliographical references and index.

  ISBN 0–231–11230–0

  1. Dead—Political aspects—Europe, Eastern.   2. Dead—Political aspects—Russia (Federation)   3. Body, Human—Symbolic aspects—Europe, Eastern.   4. Body, Human —Symbolic aspects —Russia (Federation)   5. Funeral rites and ceremonies—Europe, Eastern.   6. Funeral rites and ceremonies—Russia (Federation)   7. Ancestor worship—Europe, Eastern   8. Ancestor worship—Russia (Federation)   9. Europe, Eastern—Politics and government.   10. Russia (Federation)—Politics and government. I. Title.   II. Series: Annual W. Averell Harriman Lecture.

GT3242.V47 1999

393'.0947—dc21   98–45114

To the memory of my brother
David Simonds Verdery
untimely dead

fie-i ţărîna uşoară
neka mu je laka ʒemlja

(May the earth lie lightly on him)

And what the dead had speech for, when living
They can tell you, being dead: the communication
Of the dead is tongued with fire beyond the language of the living.

—T. S. ELIOT, "Little Gidding"

CONTENTS

ILLUSTRATIONS

FIGURES

TABLE

PREFACE AND
ACKNOWLEDGMENTS

The chapters of this book were first delivered as the W. Averell Harriman Lectures at Columbia University in, December 1997. Their title then was "Postsocialist Necrophilia, Or the Political Lives of Dead Bodies," the latter part of the word "necrophilia" having its original nonerotic Greek sense of fondness, attachment. Hence, postsocialist necrophilia: an attachment to corpses in the former socialist bloc. My aim was to investigate the numerous cases of political burials and reburials that occurred in Eastern Europe and the former Soviet Union beginning around 1989, and to ask how and why the bones and corpses of these dead people had become political symbols. My friends having convinced me that "necrophilia" was just a bit too jolly for this grave subject, I have settled (with some regret) on the present title.

In commissioning the lectures, my Columbia University hosts urged me to imagine a fairly broad audience of social scientists and humanists. Therefore I selected a topic that seemed inclusive and of potentially wide interest. I hope the book will appeal to anthropologists, political scientists, sociologists, historians, literary scholars, and nonacademics both inside and outside the area of postsocialist studies. The drawback to aiming at such a broad audience is, of course, the magnitude of the literatures relevant to my topic. In this respect I cannot claim adequate coverage of the fields whose interest I hope to attract—indeed, the point of the lectures was to explore a topic in an open-ended way, and I can certainly claim to have done that. In the course of my reading, I came upon many more interesting bits of information than I could use in the text. Finding some of them impossible to renounce, I put them in notes. I encourage readers to treat the end notes of this book as more than simply extended bibliography: they contain much that complements the text, as well as providing considerable amusement.

Why, after all, dead bodies? The subject of my lectures had several sources. The first to pique my interest, with the title of a panel at the American Ethnological Society meeting for 1990, was David William Cohen. His panelists discussed the 1989 reburial of Party Secretary Imre Nagy, leader of Hungary's 1956 uprising; the conflicts around the burial of Kenyan lawyer S. M. Otieno; the theft of Juan Perón's hands from his tomb in Argentina; and the politics of funerals in South Africa. From that experience dates the folder in my "Projects" file labeled "Political Lives of Dead Bodies." (David believes that we invented that title together and has encouraged me to use it here.) Two signal contributors to that file were Susan Gal, whose papers on the reburials of Imre Nagy and Béla Bartók showed me that something interesting was going on in post-1989 Eastern Europe, and István Rév, whose marvelous piece, "Parallel Autopsies," revealed that these reburials had a lengthy history (and that Hungary was the ultimate "necrophiliac" in the region).

I believe the impetus to turn my "Dead Bodies" folder into an actual project, however, was two events that make this by far the most personal of all my writing to date. When I was asked to give the Harriman Lectures, two and a half years had passed since the death of my father—time enough to have achieved acceptance of his death without yet having lost my sense of terrible perplexity about it. (His corpse also had considerable postmortem life, spending nearly two years at the Harvard Medical School as a teaching vehicle for future MDs [a decision to which my mother had earlier drawn him with the observation that in this way he would finally get into Harvard]). It was my family's great misfortune, however, that as I was working on the lectures, my brother died prematurely at the age of forty-six. His all-too-painful absence haunted me through every one of these pages, causing me to pose what I thought were intellectual problems that too often turned out to be emotional ones. I dedicate the work to his memory.

This book would not have been written without the impetus provided by the advisory board of Columbia University's Harriman Institute, which invited me to present the Harriman Lectures for 1997. I am grateful to those colleagues for their interest and particularly to Mark von Hagen, the institute's director, for his support and hospitality, and for making the whole event a memorable one. The Harriman family's generous endowment of the lectures permitted both stimulating exchange and a good time. In addition, I owe a large debt to the Center for Advanced Study in the Behavioral Sciences at Stanford, where I wrote the lectures. The heavenly environment there made thinking about death much more pleasant than it could possibly have been otherwise; I am grateful for the National Science Foundation Grant (#SBR-9601236) that supported my fellowship year.

I have been fortunate in all my work to enjoy the cooperation and help of many people, but never so much as in this project. Somehow the topic took over most of the professional conversations I had (during lunches, after-colloquium cocktails, E-mail exchanges, and so on), once I started work on it. Many people with whom I discussed it—far more than I can adequately acknowledge here—had useful items to contribute, while others offered valuable substantive advice. I am much indebted to Andrey Arkhipov, Pamela Ballinger, Vicki Bonnell, Michael Burawoy, Ellen Comisso, Elizabeth Dunn, Susan Gal, Ashraf Ghani, Caroline Humphrey, Anatoly Khazanov, Jeremy King, Gail Kligman, Kirstie McClure, G. William Skinner, David Stark, and Susan Woodward for their generous assistance. While I was writing the lectures at Stanford during the autumn of 1997, my work was the subject of several seminar discussions, and early drafts received useful criticism. I particularly thank the following people for this

kind of help: Ron Aminzade, Paul and Margret Baltes, Fay Cook, Lynn
Hunt, Phyllis Mack, Doug McAdam, István Rév, Laura Stoker, Sidney
Tarrow, Charles Tilly, and Dorothea von Mücke. Dr. Rév and I also
engaged in frequent conversations as I was writing the lectures and he pro-
vided a photo I have used. For additional photos I am grateful to Gerald
Creed (Dimitrov's mausoleum), Alison Fleig (Sikorski's reburial), Gail
Kligman (Statue Park), and Goranka Matić (Yugoslav dead).

Among those who offered me information and anecdotes (not all of
which I could use in the final text) about yet another dead body, I thank
Levon Abrahamian, Sorin Antohi, Wendy Bracewell, Michał Buchowski,
Silvia Colfescu, Gerald Creed, Alexander Dallin, Hermine DeSoto, Mihai
Gherman, Haldis Haukanes, Martha Lampland, Gail Lapidus, Andrew
Lass, Kitty Maguire, Kathleen Much, Maja Povrzanović, Dražen Prelec,
Bertalan Pusztai, Daina Stukuls, Ronald Suny, Maria Todorova, Frances
Trix, M. Gordon Wolman, Kathleen Young, and Marko Živković. Sidonia
Puiu and Roxana Bărbulescu provided essential research services, as well,
and Anne McCoy gave superb editorial assistance. My thanks to all of
them.

In writing about such an emotionally affecting subject, one depends
more than usual on one's friends. To those who enriched my life during
the time I wrote this book I offer my particular thanks: Paul, Fay, Lynn,
Peg, Phyllis, Jenny, Sue, Carol, Erica, Dorothea, and—most especially—
Piglet, for all those wonderful things people thank their piglets for.

THE POLITICAL LIVES
OF DEAD BODIES

Even now, Lenin is more alive than the living.
—V. V. MAIAKOVSKII[1]

INTRODUCTION

Corpses on the Move

Dead bodies have enjoyed political life the world over and since far back in time. Sophocles' *Oedipus at Colonus* tells of the contest between Thebes and Athens over the aging Oedipus, whose residence and eventual burial in one of the two cities would make of it, according to prophecy, a great city-state. Much the same thing happened with St. Francis of Assisi, whose ailing body was carted hither and yon by representatives of religious centers that hoped to get rich from housing his corpse.[2] In medieval Europe the theft of saints' relics was big business among competing holy sites.[3] We find comparable practices with cultural "saints" as well—Dante's body, for instance, was shuttled back and forth between Florence and Ravenna, according to shifting political fortunes.[4] Jean-Jacques Rousseau, Thomas Paine, and Napoleon Bonaparte are among countless political personages reburied to mark political change, and

Thomas Becket and Oliver Cromwell, two of a very large set of corpses desecrated to the same end. The reburied dead might be skeletons, or they might be actual flesh. In 1906, when Admiral John Paul Jones returned to America from Paris for a second burial, those who unsealed his casket marveled at how well-preserved he was: it seems he had been pickled in rum.[5]

More recently, in 1961 Stalin was expelled from Lenin's mausoleum, where the two had lain side by side since 1953. (At a Party Congress held well into Khrushchev's de-Stalinization campaign, a female comrade got up to report that Lenin had appeared to her in a dream and said, "It is unpleasant for me to be beside Stalin, who brought such misfortune to the party." So they took Stalin out and buried him in a far corner of the Kremlin wall.[6]) Politicized funerals and reburials paved the way to a new South Africa, as we learn from the work of historian Garrey Dennie,[7] and in Kenya's turbulent politics, lawyer S. M. Otieno spent five months in a morgue in 1987, while his widow and his clan fought in the courts for the right to bury him "properly," each side understanding that in a different way.[8]

Further examples come from Latin America. In 1990s Guatemala, exhumations and reinterments were central to democratizing politics.[9] The year 1997 saw the discovery of revolutionary hero Che Guevara, his body eagerly claimed for reburial by three different countries. (His daughter gave him to Cuba, which put him in . . . a mausoleum.) Guevara's reburial follows that of another mobile Latin American communist, Salvador Allende, reburied in 1990. Let's not forget the peripatetic Evita Perón. She died in 1952 and lay embalmed in a giant mausoleum, then accompanied her exiled husband to a secret grave site in Italy in 1955; she later followed her now-remarried spouse to Spain; finally, in 1974, her corpse returned to Argentina. Her current resting place is a sealed and triple-locked steel vault.[10] Nor did her husband, Juan Perón, rest wholly in peace: in 1987, Argentine anthropologist Rosana Guber tells us, Perón's grave was desecrated; his hands were severed from his body and stolen.[11]

When former Cambodian dictator Pol Pot died in 1998, many Cambodians felt cheated of the opportunity to bring him to justice for the terrible suffering he had inflicted. A holy man proposed taking his corpse to court and putting it on trial, in hopes of giving Cambodians some peace.[12] Somewhat more fortunate than Perón or Pol Pot was Philippine dictator Ferdinand Marcos, whom his widow Imelda stashed in a closet in a refrigerated casket, awaiting a possible homecoming. She wheeled him out for a birthday party in 1990 and later for their wedding anniversary. In 1992 Marcos was allowed to return home. He was placed in a glass coffin before an eternal flame, relaxing to tunes by Mozart—until the electric company pulled the plug on his cooled corpse for nonpayment of his music and refrigeration bills.[13]

Dead bodies are far from the only corporeal elements active in the world today: think of the sale of organs and body parts, the international adoption market, and so on. In this book, however, I limit myself to bones and corpses—not *all* bones and corpses: chiefly those that have become political symbols. I deal primarily with some politicized corpses in Eastern Europe and the former Soviet Union, particularly since 1989—hence "postsocialist" (or, if you prefer, "postcommunist"[14]). People in this region were manhandling corpses and bones quite a bit during the 1990s, more in some countries (such as Hungary and the former Yugoslavia) than in others (such as Bulgaria and eastern Germany[15]). The main questions I will explore in this book are, Why has the postsocialist period been accompanied by so much activity around dead bodies, and what does the politics concerning them signify? How does this dead-body politics differ from examples in other times and places?

This is an immense topic. To do it even minimal justice requires attending to political symbolism; to death rituals and beliefs, such as ideas about what constitutes a "proper burial"; to the connections between the particular corpses being manipulated and the wider national and international contexts of their manipulation; and to reassessing or rewriting the past and creating or retrieving "memory." Any student of dead-body politics (of which there is much, worldwide) should consider these subjects. For the former socialist bloc specifically, others are relevant, too: the shift to new democratic politics, the development of markets and the restitution of private property, the enlivening of religious worship, the creation and territorial bounding of new states. I will touch on all these intertwined themes.

In this introduction, I will show that I do indeed have a topic here, by giving evidence of dead-body manipulations in the postsocialist bloc. I will indicate the magnitude of the phenomenon by summoning up a parade of corpses from Eastern Europe and the former Soviet Union. To do so, I divide my examples into two categories: the named and famous, and the anonymous or nameless dead. The named and famous are of three kinds: statues, famous people returned from abroad, and famous locals being reburied. In chapter 1, I will offer another parade, this time of ideas with which we might think about events of this kind.

A PARADE OF DEAD BODIES

Named and Famous Dead: Statues

Take a moment to visualize the opening scene of Sergei Eisenstein's film *October*, in which the Russian proletariat tears down the statue of Tsar Alexander III during the Bolshevik Revolution. The statue is bound with ropes and a noose is placed around its neck; then it begins to rock, finally tumbling in sections from its pedestal, to the enthusiastic roars of the assembled crowd. Vividly establishing the standard iconography for moments of radical political transformation, this scene sets the stage for my first group of political corpses.

1 Statue of Tsar Alexander III being toppled in the Russian Revolution.

Statues are dead people cast in bronze or carved in stone. They symbolize a specific famous person while in a sense also *being* the body of that person. By arresting the process of that person's bodily decay, a statue alters the temporality associated with the person, bringing him into the realm of the timeless or the sacred, like an icon. For this reason, desecrating a statue partakes of the larger history of iconoclasm. Tearing it down not only removes that specific body from the landscape, as if to excise it from history, but also proves that because it can be torn down, no god protects it.[16] As it is deprived of its timelessness and sacred quality, the "sacred" of the universe in which it had meaning becomes more "profane." The person it symbolized dissolves into an ordinary, time-bound person.[17] Raising up new statues reverses the process, (re)sacralizing persons who had gone for some time unremarked. Both actions signal a change in the universe of meaning that hitherto prevailed.

Among the earliest visible signs of regime change in 1989 was that statues began falling from their pedestals, indicating the fall from favor of their fleshly counterparts. Enver Hoxha disappeared from Tirana, Albania, leaving a giant vacancy in the central square. Monuments to the Soviet "liberators" were hastily torn down all across the former satellite countries. In cities and towns throughout the region, Marx and Lenin (and even Stalin) toppled from their places (plates 2-4)—although not everywhere: Lenin still stands in Moscow's October Square, for instance; Marx hasn't yet left his post inside the former Karl Marx University in Budapest, and in Minsk and Kiev most of the heroes of socialism are still upright; East Berliners dismantled all statues of socialism's heroes except for Marx and Engels, who are mobbed by tourists (especially from Latin America).[18] Some of the dismantlings resembled veritable public executions, such as Felix Dzerzhinsky's in Warsaw. Disappeared Lenin statues have provoked much guessing as to his present location:[19] in Latvia, people submit via E-mail their answers to the contest question, "Where's Lenin?," and the matter is the subject of many jokes. Passing Lenin's empty pedestal on a Bucharest bus one day, I asked the man next to me where the statue is now (plate 5). He replied that he wasn't sure, but he'd heard it was sold to a Third World country; others said that some Japanese wanted to buy it for a museum. In Tartu, Estonia, city officials put a warehoused Lenin statue up for auction on December 5, 1997 (perhaps because of a revenue crunch?).[20] (Earlier, in 1991, the Tadjikistan parliament had voted, by contrast, to *reerect* Lenin's statue and force those who had dismantled it to pay the costs.[21]) The prize for the most original solution to the problem of what to do with all these bronze corpses goes to the Hungarians, who put the demoted statuary together in a single location outside Budapest, known as Statue Park (see plates 6–9[22]). (A similar park was later opened in Moscow.)

Meanwhile, other statues went up in their places: in Bulgaria, the bust of late-nineteenth-century politician Stefan Stambolov, renowned for maintaining order in chaotic times; in Romania, 1848 revolutionary hero Avram Iancu in place of the Monument to the Soviet Soldiers in Cluj (the soldiers were moved to the Soviet part of the town cemetery),[23] and also the fascist World War II general and head of state Ion Antonescu, executed by the communists in 1946, whose possible rehabilitation occasioned heated debate both inside Romania and with the U.S. government;[24] in Russia, statues of Tsar Nicholas and Peter the Great, as Muscovites reclaimed their tsarist past. The examples are endless.

Tearing down and erecting statues goes on all over the world, in times past as well as present; there is nothing specifically postsocialist about it. Because political order has something to do with both landscape and history, changing the political order, no matter where, often means changing the bronzed human beings who both stabilize the landscape and temporally freeze particular values in it. Although it is true that statue politics goes far beyond the postsocialist examples, there are two ways in which these instances are nonetheless specific to postsocialism.

First is their sheer number, reflecting the magnitude of the changes wrought: a far-flung social system that encompassed large numbers of people in many countries lost central features of its institutional organization (one-party rule, command economies), and in some cases federations gave way to new nation-states. Even though the social orders emerging from socialism may continue to resemble it in many respects, part of their legitimation comes from representing themselves as discontinuous with it; statue successions are critical to this representation. Second, if statues participate in stabilizing particular spatial and temporal orders, as I just suggested, then to the extent that socialism organized space and time differently from other

2 The head of Stalin (statue) on a truck.

3 The head of Lenin (statue) being removed from his body.

4 Lenin statue being taken down from its pedestal in Bucharest, Romania.

5 Lenin's empty pedestal in Bucharest.

6 Marx and Engels, from Statue Park, Budapest, Hungary.

7 Lenin in Statue Park, Budapest, Hungary.

8 Commissar and proletarian, in Statue Park.

9 A worker of the world, after losing his chains, from
Statue Park.

kinds of society, tearing down socialist-era statues is indeed special. Yampolsky argues, for example, that Soviet statues had particular qualities distinguishing them from statues in other places, in their gigantism and in the *kind* of time they froze.[25] I will not pursue this point further, other than to note that some scholars see socialism's spatial and temporal orders—and thus the statues implicated in them—as distinctive.[26]

One might object to my treating statues as part of dead-body politics, because statues clearly are not like dead bodies in a number of respects. For instance, they are almost always above ground level, burials almost always beneath it; their effect lies precisely in their permanent visibility, which most corpses lack.[27] Certainly statues and corpses differ, but some examples will show how thin is the line separating bronze from bone.[28] First, torn-down statues have often seemed to observers like dead people, as in the following comment on the removal of Felix Dzerzhinsky, founder of the Cheka and KGB, from central Moscow after the failed coup of August 1991: "[Dzerzhinsky's] statue . . . dangled from a crane, as if from a noose."[29] Dzerzhinsky's "execution" in Warsaw was similarly lifelike.[30] Second, some statues have been treated rather like actual dead bodies, their empty pedestals becoming places of pilgrimage[31] or otherwise manifesting religious and magical resonance. In Yerevan, Armenia, for example, those who took down Lenin's statue placed it on a truck and drove it as they might the body of a deceased person, round and round the central square, as if in an open coffin. Bystanders tossed onto it pine branches and coins, as they would for the dead. Still other deposed statues were placated just like newly dead persons. In Mongolia, where an immense statue of Stalin was belatedly felled in 1990, peasants sprinkled milk on the spot where the statue had stood, for they believe that this practice will prevent his angry evil spirit from returning to haunt them.[32]

Finally, two other statues became active participants in a lively dispute over whether Lenin's corpse should remain in the mausoleum in Red Square or be taken to St. Petersburg for burial. When the just-installed ten-foot statue of Tsar Nicholas II was blown to smithereens on April 1, 1997, initial speculation attributed the act to antimonarchist groups protesting proposals to rebury the imperial family and restore the monarchy. But a different group claimed responsibility, stating that theirs was "an act of retribution against those who wish to commit outrage against a *important Ex* (handwritten)

national shrine—the V. I. Lenin Mausoleum memorial complex."[33] Three
months later another such group similarly mined the just-completed statue
of Peter the Great (without, however, destroying it); they decried the
actions of "unprincipled politicians who have unleashed an odious debate
in the press over the question of reburying the body of the leader of the
world proletariat, Vladimir Ulyanov-Lenin."[34] In this way, the fates of
statues and of actual dead bodies have been thoroughly entwined.

Named and Famous Corpses

Lenin's possible departure from his mausoleum is perhaps the most widely
publicized case of postsocialist dead-body politics. I will return to him
later, but let me use him now to segue from statues to actual corpses, for
Lenin's mummy is an interesting cross between the two: it and its mausoleum have the visibility of a statue in the Moscow landscape, but the body
is located two meters below ground level, as is proper in a burial.[35] Critical
to Lenin's burial politics are his name and fame; without those, no one but
his relatives would care where he lies. The same is true of other famous
dead, whether of international or primarily local stature. Beginning with
the internationally famous, here are a few examples.

In Romania there was talk (but so far little else) of recovering from
abroad famed playwright Eugen Ionesco, philosopher Mircea Eliade, composer George Enescu, and sculptor Constantin Brâncuşi, all "local boys"
who emigrated and made the big time. More successful efforts to repatriate
similar treasures occurred in the Soviet Union, starting even before its collapse. In the late 1980s the Soviet state began a campaign to improve relations with the Russian diaspora; this included bringing back the bodies of
renowned cultural figures buried abroad. Among them was world-famous
bass Fyodor Chaliapin, who had emigrated from the Soviet Union shortly
after the Bolshevik Revolution. He surely would not have wanted to come
back to it even as a corpse, but his heirs were persuaded by the large sum of
money the Soviet government paid in order to bring him home.[36] In the late
1980s and early 1990s, skeletal musicians were definitely a popular import:
composer Béla Bartók left New York for reburial in Budapest (anthropologist Susan Gal wonderfully describes his welcome there[37]); Latvian musi-
cian Jazeps Vitols came home from Germany;[38] Poles repatriated in 1992

famed composer/politician Ignacy Jan Paderewski, who traveled to
Warsaw from Arlington National Cemetery;[39] and Czech composer
Bohuslav Martinů returned for reburial from Switzerland.[40]

Along with these world-famous sons came other exiles and émigrés
famous primarily inside their native countries.[41] Romanians retrieved
from Paris their esteemed interwar diplomat Nicolae Titulescu, and from
Rome, eighteenth-century bishop Inochentie Micu, the subject of chapter
2. Also airborne was Hungary's 1918 minister of ethnic affairs, Oszkár
Jászi, who left his tomb in Oberlin, Ohio, to return home as a Liberal
counterweight to the various Conservatives Hungary was then reburying.[42] Hungarians additionally brought back in 1992 the body of József
Cardinal Mindszenty, who had spent almost twenty-five years either in jail
or in political asylum at the U.S. embassy before accepting exile in
Austria.[43] From the United States the Czech Republic imported journalist
Ferdinand Peroutka and dramatist/actor Jiři Voskovec, and from Canada,
conductor Karel Ančerl.[44] Latvians brought home famed dissident Gunars
Astra (and are still looking for the body of their last "democratic" president, Karlis Ulmanis), who died in Soviet custody; they used the occasion
to display for the first time the flag and anthem of pre-Soviet Latvia.[45] Two
Polish generals returned home for reburial from Britain: Bor-Komorowski
(head of the Home Army in the Warsaw uprising) and Sikorski (of the
Polish government in exile)(plates 10–11).[46] A group of Croats retrieved
from the United States and reburied Vlatko Maček, head of Croatia's
interwar Peasant Party. Croatian President Tudjman, in answer to this
"provocation" by his political enemies, proposed repatriating from Italy
Ante Pavelić, leader of Croatia's World War II "ethnic cleansers," the
Ustaša.[47] (It seems that in Croatian politics, all sides need allies—dead or
alive.)

Some of these imports were not exactly skeletal. Bulgaria's last sovereign was Tsar Boris III, who died in 1943; after 1989 his widow returned
from Spain, bringing for reburial only his heart, which she had taken with
her into exile (it's not certain what happened to the rest of him).[48] Some
were ambivalent: Leo Szilard's ashes rest half in Budapest, half in upstate
New York.[49] And some of them were abortive, such as one reported by
Hungarian historian István Rév in his fascinating paper "Parallel
Autopsies." In 1989 a Hungarian furnace tycoon, convinced that he had

10 AND 11 From the reburial of General Władisław Sikorski
in Warsaw, Poland, 1993.

found in Siberia the skeleton of Hungary's illustrious 1848 revolutionary hero and poet Sándor Petőfi, determined to bring Petőfi home. He placed the skeleton in his camcorder box and (after some timely promotion of his furnaces to Siberia's residents) returned to Hungary with his prize. Unable to convince experts of the skeleton's authenticity, however—they insisted it was a young Orthodox Jewish female—he failed to obtain state sponsorship for the reburial. In the end he reburied the skeleton in his own garden.[50]

Although I have no information concerning the kind of diplomacy necessary to moving these dead across international borders, that would surely make a fascinating footnote. At the very least, we might observe of these returning dead that they help to signify a new era in East-West relations, one involving borders much more permeable than those of the communist period. (It would be interesting also to compare the imports of dead human capital from the West with the outflow of live human capital once hindered by the Iron Curtain.)

Still other corpses traveled within their home countries. Hungary seems to hold the record in this respect, and Rév recounts the adventures of a number of them. By far the most important was the reburial, in 1989, of the bones of Imre Nagy, communist prime minister at the time of Hungary's 1956 revolution; he was dug up (his bones turned out to be mixed with some giraffe bones from the Budapest Zoo), turned over, and properly reburied in a Budapest cemetery, following an enormous public commemoration.[51] I will have more to say about Nagy later. Others include communist show-trial victim László Rajk, also reburied in 1989 (having already been reburied in 1956), and Hungary's fascist leader during World War II, Admiral Horthy, who was dug up and moved to a new burial site. (His funeral, modeled on that of anti-Habsburg freedom fighter Ferencz Rákóczi, who was reburied in 1906 [see plate 12], would itself soon become the model for that of Hungary's prime minister, József Antall, who visited Horthy's grave shortly before he died.[52])

Although corpses were unusually spirited in Hungary, they were active everywhere else in Eastern Europe, too.[53] Some, like Nagy, had their hidden graves revealed. In the Czech Republic, for example, the resting place of Czechoslovak founder Tomáš Masaryk was opened to visitors; and following a reburial service, the gravestone of 1968 hero-suicide Jan Palach showed his real name, in place of the pseudonym carved there to prevent demonstrations at the grave site.[54] Other corpses moved as part of religious renewal. Besides the Romanian example in chapter 2 are several that Frances Trix reports from parts of Albania, where villagers rebuilt the shrines of Muslim mullahs whom the communists had torn from their holy places and moved to standard cemeteries. Once the new shrines were finished, the mullahs were exhumed and reinterred in their holy sites (for many of the corpses it was their third funeral).[55]

Sometimes the reburials involved treating former heads of state as quasi-religious relics. These cases almost invariably indicated struggles over the form of the polity: how much territory it should have, whether it should be a monarchy or a republic, whether or not it should acknowlege achievements of the communist period (the debates over Lenin's burial, for instance, are partly about this kind of acknowledgment). In 1989, Serbs commemorated the six hundredth anniversary of the 1389 Battle of Kosovo,

12 Reburial of Hungarian freedom fighter Ferencz Rákóczi (d. 1735) in Budapest, 1906. This reburial was the model for those of Admiral Miklós Horthy and President József Antall, Budapest, 1993.

in which Serbian Prince Lazar died and Serbia lost its autonomy to the Turks. Two years before the commemoration, in 1987, Prince Lazar's bones went on an outing prescribed by Orthodox custom. First they were taken from the patriarchate in Belgrade (the latest of several places where he had spent the last six centuries) and carried through monasteries in all the regions Serbs claim for their new state, including parts of Bosnia and Croatia; the bones then traveled to Serbia's largely Albanian province of Kosovo for burial. Prince Lazar's skeleton thus set the boundaries of greater Serbia, on the principle "Serbian land is where Serbian bones are"—even if the overwhelming *live* majority is Albanian.[56]

Another mobile monarch with saintly pretensions is Russia's Tsar Nicholas II, who together with his family was exhumed in 1991 from a secret grave site near Yekaterinburg (Sverdlovsk). Plans were made to bury them in the family crypt in St. Petersburg. When Nicholas's new statue was blown up in April 1997, however, it became clear that some people did not favor his return. Owing to fierce controversy involving Russia's communists, pro- and antimonarchists, Orthodox Church leaders, and others concerned about his body's political symbolism, the plans for reburial were canceled at least twice.[57] Meanwhile, groups in three cities—Yekaterinburg, Moscow, and St. Petersburg—vied for the honor of burying him. For months the family remained in Yekaterinburg's government pathology lab, transfixed in space by the same deadlocked political forces that held Lenin's body immobilized between St. Petersburg and his mausoleum.[58] (The chief difference is that the tsar has been proposed for canonization as a martyr, whereas sainthood is unlikely for Lenin.) Finally, on July 17, 1998 (eighty years after his execution), the tsar was properly buried in St. Petersburg in the family chapel. Politics continued to swirl about his bones even as they were interred, for the Russian patriarch declined to attend and Boris Yeltsin came only at the last minute.

A third ambulatory monarch, less saintly than patriotic, is Frederick the Great; his travels (like those of Prince Lazar) helped to define a new state territory. After Germany's reunification, his remains, together with those of his dog, were taken from Castle Hohenzollern in Baden-Württemberg (former West Germany) to Sans Souci, his palace in Potsdam (former East Germany), whence they had been hastily removed at the close of World War II and spirited out to the Allied-occupied West. Returning Frederick to Prussia—an event supported if not indeed initiated by Chancellor Kohl—showed that Germany was no longer divided by internal barriers to the rejoining of Prussian traditions with modern West Germany.[59]

Not all corpse transfers indicated, as do many of the above, resuscitated honor: sometimes quite the reverse.[60] Communist mausoleums sent out eviction notices, as did the Kremlin wall. While Lenin's fate hung in the balance, top Romanian Party leaders of the past were removed from their mausoleum and sent to grave sites that were more humble. Stalin, already exiled from the Lenin mausoleum in 1961, is pondering yet another move, this time to his native Georgia.[61] After the Bulgarian Socialist Party's victory in the 1990 elections, Bulgaria's opposition defaced the mausoleum of mummified communist leader Georgi Dimitrov (plate 13); his family secretly removed and cremated his body, fearing its desecration.[62]

What unites all these mobile corpses with each other as well as with the statues discussed above is their renown. By repositioning them, restoring them to honor, expelling them, or simply drawing attention to them, their exit from one grave and descent into another mark a change in social visibilities and values, part of the larger process of postsocialist transformation. Precisely because at the time of their deaths these men had

13 Defaced mausoleum of Georgi Dimitrov, Sofia, Bulgaria.

achieved visibility around certain values, which then receded or were suppressed, handling them recalls those values in contrast to the ones lately
prevailing. Demoting the corpses and statues of the "visibles" of socialism does the reverse. Parading the dead bodies of famous men thus uses
their specific biographies to reevaluate the national past.

Anonymous Dead

Other ways of accomplishing this reevaluation involve reburying or otherwise drawing attention to the nameless, known only to their families,
friends, and neighbors. Through them, not individual/national biographies but entire social categories ("fascists," a specific generation, "Serbs,"
etc.) are repositioned or associated with different sets of values. Dead-
body politics of this sort have the important effect of inserting such
reevaluation directly into the lives of persons, families, and small groups,
through visceral processes of reburial and grieving or even vengeance.
The political consequences of such events depend on variations in the
numbers and kinds of nameless dead and the causes of their deaths.

Most numerous among the nameless dead are victims of communist
persecution and people killed during World War II. In Romania, for
instance, wide publicity accompanied the discovery of several mass burials, their victims thought to be people imprisoned by the communists, victims of Secret Police torture, those who died during forced labor on the
Danube Canal (Romania's gulag), and so on. Similar collective grave sites
have appeared throughout Russia, especially near prisons or labor
camps,[63] and are found elsewhere in the region. Seeking to retrieve loved
ones who disappeared in the early years of communist rule has been a
painful but cathartic experience that generally intensifies for its participants the rejection of communist-era values.[64]

Policies became heated over nameless dead from World War II. In
Poland, momentous political changes pivoted on a dispute with the Soviet
Union over who had in fact slaughtered the World War II Polish officers
buried in Katyń forest and other mass graves. Gorbachev officially
announced in 1990 that it was not the Nazis who had done the deed, as
Soviet leaders had long insisted, but Soviet troops.[65] Nameless dead also
played a significant part in declarations or wars of independence. In

Ukraine and Belarus, the discovery of mass grave sites full of anonymous Ukrainians and Belarusians massacred by Russians impelled those two republics toward secession from the Soviet Union.[66] The most extreme instance of dead-body politics involving nameless World War II dead, however, is Yugoslavia. Entire battalions of them served as "shock troops" in the Yugoslav breakup; from limestone caves, rival ethnic groups exhumed hundreds of skeletons, brandishing them as World War II victims of the first "ethnic cleansing." Mass graves remain a shattering reality of the Yugoslav wars in the 1990s, as well (I will return to them in chapter 3).

A parade of dead bodies indeed! And these are far from the only corpses on the move in the postsocialist bloc.[67]

CONCLUSION

How should we think about phenomena like these? Are they a form of "spectre succession," with ghosts returning to banish decisively that famous spectre Karl Marx identified 150 years ago, the "spectre of Communism"? Are we witnessing a rejuvenation of imagery from Dracula, as the seeming dead arise from the grave, some for the severalth time? Perhaps the more appropriate imagery is Taussig's "spirit possession," as a foundational act of new states.[68] Do the politics surrounding dead people simply trade on death metaphors in order to talk about the demise of the world communist system? (This tactic is common in the popular press: think of books such as Robert Kaplan's *Balkan Ghosts: A Journey Through History* and Tina Rosenberg's *The Haunted Land: Facing Europe's Ghosts After Communism.*) The mock funeral procession in downtown Sofia in 1997, for instance, in which Bulgarian students bore a coffin with the corpse of communism, suggests that interpretation. Given the evidence of active corpses in many places besides the postsocialist world, how can we characterize the specificity of current examples from that region, compared with others elsewhere? *Are* they specific or unusual in some way?

Those of you who hope for a single answer to these questions or a single explanation encompassing the varied instances will leave this book unsatisfied. To begin with, anthropologists are not good at producing that kind of account; we have too lively an awareness of cultural variation and of what Gillian Feeley-Harnik calls "life's abiding murkiness."[69] Occam's razor is not our favorite truth instrument, for it shaves off all the interesting particulars. Second, as is often observed, although death is the great universal, it calls forth human responses that are extraordinarily varied. The fact that people are everywhere digging up and reburying other people does not mean that all those instances have the same sense. Agreeing with Reinhart Koselleck in his book *The Political Cult of the Dead*, I work from the assumption that although such phenomena have broad similarities internationally, their political meanings are more localized.[70] The form may seem constant, yet each case has its own uniqueness.

My task in what follows is to explore some of those uniquenesses and at the same time to seek commonalities among these postsocialist cases. In the first chapter I offer some framing concepts that I find fruitful for thinking about the political lives of dead bodies; in chapters 2 and 3, I give two extended examples to illustrate those points. My overall argument underscores the role of dead bodies in animating postsocialist politics, as people struggle to come to terms with the profound changes in their environments and their universes of meaning that have ensued from the events of 1989.

Dead people belong to the live people who claim them most obsessively.
—JAMES ELLROY

CHAPTER ONE

Dead Bodies Animate the Study of Politics

*I*n my introduction I revealed a lively politics around dead bodies during the 1990s in the former Soviet bloc. My task now is to indicate what I plan to make of it. As I already noted, I approach the task mindful of its complexity and unwilling to offer a single explanation of the varied instances I have presented. What I offer, instead, is a broad framework for thinking about material of this kind, one that emphasizes the universes of meaning within which postsocialist politics takes place.

I see politics as a form of concerted activity among social actors, often involving stakes in particular goals. These goals may be contradictory, sometimes only quasi-intentional; they can include making policy, justifying actions taken, claiming authority and disputing the authority claims of others, and creating or manipulating the cultural categories within which all of those activities are pursued. Politics is not restricted to the actions of political leaders but can be engaged in by anyone, although such actors often seek to present their goals as in some sense *public* ones.[1] That is, some of the work of politics consists of making claims that create an issue as a "public" issue. Political actors pursue their activities in arenas both large and small, public and private; the overlap and interference of the arenas shape what goes on in any one of them. Because human activity nearly always has affective and meaningful dimensions and takes place through complex symbolic processes, I also view politics as a realm of continual struggles over meanings, or signification. Therefore, I stress those aspects in my discussion, and I find dead bodies a particularly good vehicle for doing so.

Politics happens in contexts. Because the context of postsocialist politics is unusually momentous, I preface my discussion with a brief sketch of what I think it is. I start with the assumption that for the last two decades or so, we have been both creating and living through an epochal shift in the global economy. Among its elements is a change in the operation of capitalism, responding to a global recession evident as of the early 1970s. A large literature, beyond my purposes here, has arisen around this transformation. Sometimes called a change to "flexible specialization,"[2] it has produced a massive shift in the tectonic plates of the world economy; one sign of that was the 1989 collapse of Communist Party rule in Eastern Europe, and soon thereafter in the Soviet Union. I have suggested elsewhere how I think that happened, underscoring processes internal to the Soviet system that connected it more fully with international capital flows and, as a result, altered both the form of socialist political economies and their place in global capitalism.[3]

Although I am not alone in seeing the postsocialist transformation in such earthshaking terms, my view is far from universal. Some observers find increasing evidence that as the dust from 1989 settles, persistent continuities with the socialist order are at least as striking as disruptions of it. The centralized economy and socialist property rights, in particular, have proved highly resistant to change. Nevertheless, much of what set socialism most clearly apart from other forms of political economy was wholly compromised after 1989: the Communist Party's relative monopoly over the formal political sphere, the degree of central control over the budget and over economic redistribution, the mechanisms that sustained socialist property as the dominant form, and the illusion of the party-state's omnipotence (brought into question by Poland's Solidarity in 1980 but smashed altogether in 1989). Even if some of these features continue in postsocialist societies, they no longer index the distinctive cluster of institutions that was "actually existing socialism."

Moreover, the context in which those features operate has changed. The various barriers that socialism had fumblingly erected no longer insulate it from the "outside." Global capitalism exerts its pressure particularly against the institutions by which socialism defined itself as noncapitalist, such as party and state forms, property arrangements, and openness to market forces. Although the results of outside pressure will not necessarily be "transitions to capitalism," the context in which we should assess postsocialism's emerging forms is—far more than before—the international one of global capital flows. When I speak of a shift in the world's "tectonic plates," then, I do not mean that a plate called "socialism" has buckled before one called "capitalism"; I mean, rather, that an alteration in the entire system of plate movements compels us to reconsider the dynamics in any one part of it. For the postsocialist part, those dynamics affect the full gamut of politicoeconomic and sociocultural life.

Where do dead bodies figure in this? I believe they offer us some purchase on the cultural dimension, in the anthropological sense, of postsocialist politics. (By this I do not mean the so-called concept of political culture, as underspecified as it is overused.[4]) They help us to see political transformation as something more than a technical process—of introducing democratic procedures and methods of electioneering, of forming political parties and nongovernmental organizations, and so on. The "something more" includes meanings, feelings, the sacred, ideas of morality, the nonrational—all ingredients of "legitimacy" or "regime consolidation" (that dry phrase), yet far broader than what analyses employing those terms usually provide. Through dead bodies, I hope to show how we might think about politics, both as strategies and maneuvering and also as activity occurring within cultural systems.

Hinted at in my wording is a view similar to Max Weber's: that the pursuit of meaning is at the heart of human activity, and that social analysis aims to understand meanings rather than to explain causes. In his work, Weber described some overarching processes he believed characteristic of modernity, such as rationalization, secularization, and the "disenchantment" of the world. In hands other than his, however, such concepts have

tended to desiccate how politics is treated. I prefer, in examining postsocialist politics, to speak instead of its *enchantment*, so as to enliven politics
with a richer sense of what it might consist of.[5]

In speaking of enchantment or enlivening, I have two related things in
mind. The first is an analytic one: I hope to show how we might animate the
study of *politics in general*, energizing it with something more than the
opinion polls, surveys, analyses of "democratization indices," and game-
theoretic formulations that dominate so much of the field of comparative
politics.[6] Where else, I ask, might we look for "politics," in perhaps unexpected places that arrest the imagination? The second sense is a descriptive
one, concerning the specific forms that political action is taking in the postsocialist world. Do we find there the ritual murders, pyramid schemes, and
images of zombies and clandestinely circulating body parts described, for
example, by Jean and John Comaroff in their work on postapartheid South
Africa?[7] Perhaps not, but we do find UFO movements in Armenia, invocations of the devil as a source of wealth in Transylvania, and radio-based
mass hypnotism in Russia.[8] My two senses of enchantment (the analytic
and the descriptive) are interconnected: we more easily broaden our conception of "the political" in the face of empirical surprises like those.

The analytic and descriptive senses are also, however, importantly distinct. In trying to animate or enchant the study of politics, I am not saying
that secular socialism dried out a politics that must now be reinfused with
meaning (or even "reborn," as some would have it[9]). To the contrary: communist parties strove continually, as Jowitt has argued, to establish their
sacrality and charisma.[10] Rather, I am protesting that perhaps from too
much rational choice theory, our standard conception of "the political" has
become narrow and flat. Therefore, I propose turning things around:
instead of seeing nationalism, for instance, in the usual way—as a matter
of territorial borders, state-making, "constructionism," or resource competition—I see it as part of kinship, spirits, ancestor worship, and the cir-
culation of cultural treasures. Rather than speak of legitimacy, I speak of
reordering the meaningful universe. I present the politics of corpses as
being less about legitimating new governments (though it can be that, too)
than about cosmologies and practices relating the living and the dead. And
I see the rewriting of history that is obviously central to dead-body politics
as part of a larger process whereby fundamental changes are occurring in

conceptions of time itself. These are the kinds of things I mean when I speak of analytically enlivening or enchanting politics.*

Investigating the political lives of dead bodies, then, enriches our sense of the political while providing a window onto its specific forms in the transformation of socialism. The rest of this book offers some examples of how such an analysis might proceed. A number of themes contribute to the enlivened sense of politics that I am advocating, and most of this chapter is devoted to discussing them. Before I continue, however, I believe I must raise a difficult question, albeit with only tentative answers: Why dead bodies? What is it about a corpse that seems to invite its use in politics, especially in moments of major transformation?

WHY DEAD BODIES?

To ask this question exposes one to a flourishing literature on "the body," much of it inspired by feminist theory and philosophy,[11] as well as potentially to poststructuralist theories about language and "floating signifiers." I will not take up the challenge of this literature here but will limit myself instead some observations about bodies as symbolic vehicles that I think illuminate their presence in postsocialist politics.[12]

Bones and corpses, coffins and cremation urns, are material objects. Most of the time, they are indisputably *there*, as our senses of sight, touch, and smell can confirm. As such, a body's materiality can be critical to its symbolic efficacy: unlike notions such as "patriotism" or "civil society," for instance, a corpse can be moved around, displayed, and strategically located in specific places. Bodies have the advantage of concreteness that nonetheless transcends time, making past immediately present. Their "thereness" undergirded the founding and continuity of medieval monasteries, providing tangible evidence of a monastery's property right to donated lands.[13] That is, their corporeality makes them important means

---

* I alternate among these words and others like "animate" or "enrich," rather than resting with the word "enchant," hoping thereby to make my meaning clearer. One might too easily read "enchant" to imply fairy tales and magic; although in postsocialism we indeed find some of that, I have in mind something a bit more down-to-earth.

of *localizing* a claim (something they still do today, as I suggest in chapter 3). They state unequivocally, as Peter Brown notes, *"Hic locus est."*[14] This quality also grounded their value as relics.

The example of relics, however, immediately complicates arguments based on the body's materiality: if one added together all the relics of St. Francis of Assisi, for instance, one would get rather more than the material remains of one dead man. So it is not a relic's actual derivation from a specific body that makes it effective but people's belief in that derivation. In short, the significance of corpses has less to do with their concreteness than with how people think about them. A dead body is meaningful not in itself but through culturally established relations to death and through the way a specific dead person's importance is (variously) construed.[15] Therefore, I turn to the properties of corpses that make them, in Lévi-Strauss's words, "good to think" as symbols.

Bodies—especially those of political leaders—have served in many times and places worldwide as symbols of political order. Literature in both historiography and anthropology is rife with instances of a king's death calling into question the survival of the polity. More generally, political transformation is often symbolized through manipulating bodies (cutting off the head of the king, removing communist leaders from mausoleums). We, too, exhibit this conception, in idioms such as "the body politic."

A body's symbolic effectiveness does not depend on its standing for one particular thing, however, for among the most important properties of bodies, especially dead ones, is their ambiguity, multivocality, or polysemy. Remains are concrete, yet protean; they do not have a single meaning but are open to many different readings. Because corpses suggest the lived lives of complex human beings, they can be evaluated from many angles and assigned perhaps contradictory virtues, vices, and intentions. While alive, these bodies produced complex behaviors subject to much debate that produces further ambiguity. As with all human beings, one's assessment of them depends on one's disposition, the context one places them in (brave or cowardly compared with whom, for instance), the selection one makes from their behaviors in order to outline their "story," and so on. Dead people come with a curriculum vitae or résumé—several possible résumés, depending on which aspect of their life is being considered. They lend themselves to analogy with *other people's* résumés. That is, they encourage identification with their life story, from several possible vantage points. Their complexity makes it fairly easy to discern different sets of emphasis, extract different stories, and thus rewrite history. Dead bodies have another great advantage as symbols: they don't talk much on their own (though they did once). Words can be put into their mouths—often quite ambiguous words—or their own actual words can be ambiguated by quoting them out of context. It is thus easier to rewrite history with dead people than with other kinds of symbols that are speechless.

Yet because they have a single name and a single body, they present the illusion of having *only one* significance. Fortifying that illusion is their materiality, which implies their having a single meaning that is solidly "grounded," even though in fact they have no such single meaning. Different people can invoke corpses as symbols, thinking those corpses mean the same thing to all present, whereas in fact they may mean different things to each. All that is shared is everyone's *recognition* of this dead person as somehow important. In other words, what gives a dead body symbolic effectiveness in politics is precisely its ambiguity, its capacity to evoke a variety of understandings.[16] Let me give an example.

On June 16, 1989, a quarter of a million Hungarians assembled in downtown Budapest for the reburial of Imre Nagy, Hungary's communist prime minister at the time of the 1956 revolution.[17] For his attempts to reform socialism he had been hanged in 1958, along with four members of his government, and buried with them in unmarked graves, without coffins, facedown. From the Hungarian point of view, this is a pretty ignominious end.[18] Yet now he and those executed with him were reburied, faceup in coffins, with full honors and with tens of thousands in attendance. Anyone watching Hungarian television on that June 16 would have seen a huge, solemn festivity, carefully orchestrated, with many foreign dignitaries as well as three Communist Party leaders standing near the coffins (the Communist Party of Hungary had not yet itself become a corpse). The occasion definitely looked official (in fact it was organized privately), and it rewrote the history—given only one official meaning for forty years—of Nagy's relation to the Hungarian people (see plates 14-15).[19]

14 AND 15 Scenes from the reburial of Imre Nagy, Budapest, 16 June 1989.

Although the media presented a unified image of him, there was no consensus on what Nagy's reburied corpse in fact meant. Susan Gal, analyzing the political rhetoric around the event, finds five distinct clusters of imagery, some of it associated with specific political parties or groups:[20] (1) nationalist images emphasizing national unity around a hero of the nation (nationalist parties soon found these very handy); (2) religious images (which could be combined with the nationalist ones) emphasizing rebirth, reconciliation, and forgiveness, and presenting Nagy as a martyr rather than a hero; (3) various images of him as a communist, as the first reform communist, and as a true man of the people, his reburial symbolizing the triumph of a humane socialist option and the death of a cruel Stalinist one; (4) generational images, presenting him as the symbol of the younger generation whose life chances had been lost with his execution (this group would soon become the Party of Young Democrats); and (5) images associated with the ideas of truth, conscience, and rehabilitation, so that his reburial signified clearing one's name and telling the story of one's persecution—an opportunity to rewrite one's personal history. (That some people presented communist Prime Minister Nagy as an *anti*communist hero shows just how complex his significances could be.)

Perhaps attendance at Nagy's funeral was so large, then, because he brought together diverse segments of the population, all resonating differently to various aspects of his life. And perhaps so many political formations were able to participate because all could legitimate a claim of some kind through him, even though the claims themselves varied greatly.[21] This, it seems to me, is the mark of a good political symbol: it has legitimating effects not because everyone agrees on its meaning but because it compels interest *despite* (because of?) divergent views of what it means.

Aside from their evident materiality and their surfeit of ambiguity, dead bodies have an additional advantage as symbols: they evoke the awe, uncertainty, and fear associated with "cosmic" concerns, such as the meaning of life and death.[22] For human beings, death is the quintessential cosmic issue, one that brings us all face to face with ultimate questions about what it means to be—and to stop being—human, about where we have come from and where we are going. For this reason, corpses lend themselves particularly well to politics in times of major upheaval, such as the postsocialist period. The revised status of religious institutions in postsocialist Eastern Europe reinforces that connection, for religions have long specialized in dealing with ultimate questions. Moreover, religions monopolize the practices associated with death, including both formal notions of burial and the "folk superstitions" that all the major faiths so skillfully integrated into their rituals. Except in the socialist period, East Europeans over two millennia have associated death with religious practices. A religious reburial nourishes the dead person both with these religious associations and with the rejection of "atheist" communism. Politics around a reburied corpse thus benefits from the aura of sanctity the corpse is presumed to bear, and from the implicit suggestion that a reburial (re)sacralizes the political order represented by those who carry it out.

Their sacred associations contribute to another quality of dead bodies as symbols: their connection with affect, a significant problem for social analysis. Anthropologists have long asked, Wherein lies the efficacy of symbols? How do they engage emotions?[23] The same question troubles other social sciences as well: Why do some things and not others work emotionally in the political realm? It is asked particularly about symbols used to evoke national identifications; Benedict Anderson, for instance, inquires why national meanings command such deep emotional responses and why people are "ready to die for these inventions."[24] The link of dead bodies to the sacred and the cosmic—to the feelings of awe aroused by contact with death—seems clearly part of their symbolic efficacy.

One might imagine that another affective dimension to corpses is their being not just any old symbol: unlike a tomato can or a dead bird, they were once human beings with lives that are to be valued. They are heavy symbols because people cared about them when they were alive, and identify with them. This explanation works best for contemporary deaths, such as the Yugoslav ones I discuss in chapter 3. Many political corpses, however, were known and loved in life by only a small circle of people; or—like Serbia's Prince Lazar or Romania's bishop Inochentie Micu (whose case I examine in the next chapter)—they lived so long ago that any feelings they arouse can have nothing to do with them as loved individuals. Therefore I find it insufficient to explain their emotional efficacy merely by their having been human beings.

Perhaps more to the point is their ineluctable self-referentiality as symbols: because all people have bodies, any manipulation of a corpse directly enables one's identification with it through one's own body, thereby tapping into one's reservoirs of feeling. In addition (or as a result), such manipulations may mobilize preexisting affect by evoking one's own personal losses or one's identification with specific aspects of the dead person's biography. This possibility increases wherever national ideologies emphasize ideas about suffering and victimhood, as do nearly all in Eastern Europe.[25] These kinds of emotional effects are likely enhanced when death's "ultimate questions," fear, awe, and personal identifications are experienced in public settings—for example, mass reburials like those of Imre Nagy or the Yugoslav skeletons from World War II.

Finally, I believe the strong affective dimension of dead-body politics also stems from ideas about kinship and proper burial. Kinship notions are powerful organizers of feeling in all human societies; other social forms (such as national ideologies) that harness kinship idioms profit from their power. Ideas about proper burial often tie kinship to cosmic questions concerning order in the universe, as well. I will further elaborate on this suggestion later in this chapter and in chapter 3.

Dead bodies, I have argued, have properties that make them particularly effective political symbols. They are thus excellent means for accumulating something essential to political transformation: symbolic capital.[26] (Given the shortage of investment capital in postsocialist countries and the difficulties of economic reform, perhaps the symbolic variety takes on special significance!) The fall of communist parties devalued much of what had served as political or symbolic capital, opening a wide field for competition in which success depends on finding and accumulating new capital resources. Dead bodies, in short, can be a site of political profit. In saying this, I am partly talking about the process of establishing political legitimacy, but by emphasizing symbolic capital I mean to keep at the forefront of my discussion the symbolic elements of that process.

REORDERING WORLDS OF MEANING

In considering the symbolic properties of corpses, I have returned repeatedly to their "cosmic" dimension.[27] I do so because I believe this emphasis suits what I observed earlier about the significance of the events of 1989:

they mark an epochal shift in the international system, one whose effects pose fundamental challenges to people's hitherto meaningful existence. This is true worldwide, but especially in the former socialist bloc. All human beings act within certain culturally shaped background expectations and understandings, often not conscious, about what "reality" is.[28] One might call these their sense of cosmic order, or their general understanding of their place in the universe.[29] By this I mean, for instance, ideas about where people in general and our people in particular came from; who are the most important kinds of people, and how one should behave with them; what makes conduct moral or immoral; what are the essential attributes of a "person"; what is time, and how does it flow (or not); and so on.

Following current anthropological wisdom, however, I do not see these cosmic conceptions strictly as "ideas," in the cognitive realm alone. Rather, they are inseparable from action in the world—they are beliefs and ideas materialized in action. This is one way (the way I prefer) of defining culture. Unfortunately, nearly all nonanthropologists understand "culture" as cognition, ideas—a meaning I want to avoid.[30] Hence, instead of using "culture," I speak of "worlds of meaning" or simply "worlds" (though *not* in the sense of "lifeworld" that is specific to phenomenology and the recent work of Jürgen Habermas). "World," as I intend it, seeks to capture a combination of "worldview" and associated action-in-the-world, people's sense of a meaningful universe in which they also act. Their ideas and their action constantly influence one another in a dynamic way. In moments of major transformation, people may find that new forms of action are more productive than the ones they are used to, or that older forms make sense in a different way, or that ideals they could only aspire to before are now realizable. Such moments lead to reconfiguring one's world; the process can be individual and collective, and it is often driven by the activities of would-be elites (in competition with one another).

Students of the demise of Soviet-style party-states have tended to pose the problems of postsocialist transformation as creating markets, making private property, and constructing democracy. This frame permits two things: one can absorb the postsocialist examples into a worldwide "transition to democracy," and one can emphasize technical solutions to the difficulties encountered ("shock therapy," writing constitutions, election-management consulting, training people in new ways of bookkeeping, etc.). I believe the postsocialist change is much bigger. It is a problem of reorganization on a cosmic scale, and it involves the redefinition of virtually everything, including morality, social relations, and basic meanings. It means a reordering of people's entire meaningful worlds.[31]

Although my phrasing may seem exaggerated, without this perspective I doubt that we can grasp the magnitude of what 1989 has meant for those living through it: a rupture in their worlds of meaning, their sense of cosmic order. The end of Party rule was a great shock to people living in the former socialist countries. This was not because everyone had internalized the Communist Party's own cosmology and organization of things: far from it. The history of Party rule throughout the region was a long struggle between what Party leaders wanted and what everyone else was prepared to live with. Practices, expectations, and beliefs quite antithetical to the Party's dictates jostled with those the Party promoted. Nevertheless, daily life proceeded within or against certain constraints, opportunities, and rules of the game that the political system had established, and these formed a set of background expectations framing people's lives.

The events of 1989 disrupted these background expectations in ways that many people in the region found disorienting (even if some of them also found therein new opportunities). They could no longer be sure what to say in what contexts, how to conduct politics with more than one political party, how to make a living in the absence of socialist subsidies and against spiraling inflation, and so on. They found their leisurely sense of time's passage wholly unsuited to the sudden crunch of tasks they had to do. Moreover, their accustomed relations with other people became suddenly tense. Quarrels over property, for example, severed long-amicable bonds between siblings and neighbors; new possibilities for enrichment altered friendships; and increasing numbers of parents saw their plans for security and retirement evaporate as more of their children headed abroad. In these circumstances, people of all kinds could no longer count on their previous grasp of how the world works. Whether consciously or not, they became open to reconsidering (either on their own or with the help of political, cultural, and religious elites) their social relations and their worlds of meaning. This is what I mean when I speak of reordering meaningful worlds. I believe dead-body politics plays a part in that process, and that to examine it will clarify my project of animating the study of politics.

My conceptualization here resonates with Durkheim's, particularly the Durkheim of the *Elementary Forms of the Religious Life*, which is among other things a treatise on the possibilities for moral regeneration in human societies.[32] The resemblance is not fortuitous. First, Durkheim wrote during a time of great moral ferment in France; his work aimed expressly to comment upon that ferment and contribute to quieting it. His situation then reminds one of the 1990s postsocialist situation. Second (and for that very reason), some scholars consider Durkheim the only major theorist apt for thinking about political and moral renewal.[33] Although I gladly second him in that endeavor, and although some of my proposals in this book (such as the theme of proper burial) hint at a Durkheimian reflex, I part company with him in regard to the *conscience collective*; I look not for *shared* mentalities but for *conflict* among groups over social meanings.

Reordering worlds can consist of almost anything—that's what a "world" means. To reorder worlds of meaning implicates all realms of activity: social relations, political ideas and behavior, worldviews, economic action. Far more domains of life might be included under this rubric than I have time to explore, and dead bodies can serve as loci for struggling over new meanings in any of them. For my purposes in this book, I will emphasize their role in the following areas: struggles to endow authority and politics with sacrality or a "sacred" dimension; contests over what might make the postsocialist order a moral one; competing politicizations of space and time; and reassessments of identities (especially national ones) and social relations. I discuss a fifth possible domain central to postsocialist transformation—property relations—together with the others, for it enters into all of them. Yet another domain that figures centrally in Eastern Europe's transformation but cannot be treated here is the obverse of death, namely [re]birth. The politics of abortion, for instance, has agitated nearly all postsocialist countries, as pro-natalist nationalists strive for demographic renewal of their nations following what they see to be socialism's "murderous" abortion policies.[34]

In each of these domains, dead bodies serve as sites of political conflict related to the process of reordering the meaningful universe. The conflicts involve elites of many kinds and the populations they seek to influence, in the altered balance of power that characterizes the period since 1989. I will explain what I intend by these rubrics, briefly for the first three and at greater length for the fourth.

Authority, Politics, and the Sacred

The meaningful worlds of human beings generally include sets of values concerning authority—values like the monarch's divinity, orderly bureaucratic procedure, a leader's charisma, full democratic participation, the scientific laws of progress, and so on. Like Weber, we can speak of different ways of acknowledging authority as modes of legitimation, and in considering social change we can ask how one group of legitimating values gives way to another. Unlike Weber, who tended to see the sacred as part of only some modes of authority, I (and many other anthropologists) would hold that authority *always* has a "sacred" component, even if it is reduced merely to holding "as sacred" certain secular values. This was certainly true of socialist regimes, which sought assiduously to sacralize themselves as guardians of secular values, especially the scientific laws of historical progress. Because their language omitted notions of the sacred, however, both outsiders and their own populations tended to view them as lacking a sacred dimension.[35]

Part of reordering meaningful worlds since 1989, then, is to sacralize authority and politics in new ways. A ready means of presenting the postsocialist order as something different from before has been to reinsert expressly sacred values into political discourse. In many cases, this has meant a new relation between religion and the state, along with a renewal of religious faith.[36] Reestablishing faith or relations with a church enables both political parties and individuals to symbolize their anticommunism and their return to precommunist values. This replaces the kind of sacredness that undergirded the authority of communist parties and serves to sacralize politics in new ways. In chapter 2 I describe a conflict that has arisen around the connection of church with politics in Romania (and other Orthodox countries). Among the conflict's many facets are struggles over the sacralization of politics, and reburying a dead body is part of them.

Moral Order

Use of religious idioms may also be part of remaking the world as a *moral* place. Because communist parties proclaimed themselves custodians of a particular moral order, the supersession of communism reopens concepts of political morality, both for politicians and others who want to claim it, and for ordinary citizens concerned with the behavior of those they live among. In the first few years following 1989, the route to new moral orders passed chiefly through stigmatizing the communist one: all who presented themselves either as opposed to communism or as its victims were ipso facto making a moral claim.

Many of these claims led to attempts at assessing blame or accountability and at achieving revenge, compensation, or restitution. Depending on who organizes and executes the process, the moral order implied in pursuing accountability can strengthen a new government, garner international support for a party to a dispute, or restore dignity to individual victims and their families. Society's members may see enforcing accountability as part of moral "purification": the guilty are no longer shielded, the victims can tell of their suffering, and the punishment purifies a public space that the guilty had made impure. Alternatively, the moral outcome may be seen as lying not in purification but in compensation for wrongs acknowledged. Foremost among the means for this was the question of restoring private property ownership, as something *morally essential* to a new anticommunist order. Efforts to establish accountability thus served to draw up a moral balance sheet, to settle accounts, as a condition of making the postsocialist order a moral one. Assessing blame and demanding accountability can occur at many sites, one of them being dead bodies. (In chapter 3, I discuss a particularly stark instance of this, former Yugoslavia, where rival exhumations produced reciprocal charges of genocide and acts of revenge that fueled the breakup of the Yugoslav state.)

Another form of "accounting" that implicates dead bodies involves efforts to determine "historical truth," which many accuse socialism of having suppressed. An example is the reburial of Imre Nagy, mentioned above, which sought to reestablish historical truth about Nagy's place in Hungarian history, as part of creating a new moral universe. His example leads us to an additional means of reordering worlds, namely, giving new values to space and time.

Reconfiguring Space and Time

As scholars ranging from Durkheim to Elias to Leach have argued, what we call space and time are social constructs.[37] All human societies show characteristic ways of conceptualizing and organizing them; any one society may contain multiple ways, perhaps differentiated by activity or social group.[38] When I speak of how space and time can be resignified, I have in mind two distinct possibilities: the more modest one of changing how space and time are marked or punctuated, and the more momentous one of transforming spatiality and temporality themselves. Socialism attempted both, the latter by imposing entirely new rules on the uses of space and creating temporalities that were arrhythmic and apocalyptic instead of the cyclical and linear rhythms they displaced.[39] I will leave that subject to chapter 3 and will briefly discuss changes in temporal and spatial punctuation now.

We might think of both space and time using the metaphor of a geological landscape. Any landscape contains more potential landmarks than are noted by those who pass through it. When I speak of "punctuating" or "marking" space and time, I mean highlighting a specific set of landmarks—using this rock or that hill (or date, or event) as a point of reference, instead of some other rock or hill (or date or event), or some other feature altogether, such as a railway crossing. Influencing the kinds of features selected are such things as one's position relative to them (a rock is a useful landmark only from a certain angle or distance), cultural factors (some groups find trees more meaningful than rocks), local economies (hunter-gatherers will notice items a traveling salesman will miss), and so on. If we put our landscape on "fast forward," the landscape itself transforms, hills and mountains rising up or subsiding while valleys are etched and floras change type. The constantly changing relief presents still other possibilities for establishing landmarks. I think of such spatiotemporal landmarks as aspects of people's meaningful worlds; modifying the landmarks is part of reordering those worlds.

For example, as I observed in the introduction, among the most common ways in which political regimes mark space are by placing particular statues in particular places and by renaming landmarks such as streets, public squares, and buildings. These provide contour to landscapes, socializing them and saturating them with specific political values: they *signify* space in specific ways. Raising and tearing down statues gives new values to space (resignifies it), just as does renaming streets and buildings. Another form of resignifying space comes from changes in property ownership, which may require adding border stones and other markers to differentiate land-scapes that socialism had homogenized. Where the political change includes creating entire nation-states, as in ex-Yugoslavia and parts of the Soviet Union, resignifying space extends further: to marking territories as "ours" and setting firm international borders to distinguish "ours" from "theirs." The location of those borders is part of the politics of space, and dead bodies have been active in it.

As for time, among the usual ways of altering its political values are by creating wholly new calendars, as in the French Revolution (whose first casualties included clocks themselves[40]); by establishing holidays to punc-tuate time differently; by promoting activities that have new work rhythms or time discipline; and by giving new contours to the "past" through revising genealogies and rewriting history.[41] Since 1989, the last of these has been very prominent in "overcoming" the socialist past and (as some people see it) returning to a "normal" history. I view this histor-ical revision, too, as an aspect of reordering worlds, and one important means of doing it has been to reposition dead bodies.

National Identities and Social Relations

The worlds of meaning that human beings inhabit include characteristic organizations of what we call "identities."[42] In the contemporary United States, people are thought to hold several identities, the most commonly mentioned being class, occupation, race, gender, and ethnic identity; in other times and places, these would have been less salient than kin-based identifications, or rank in a system of feudal estates. Especially prominent in the East European region have been national identifications. Contrary to popular opinion, I and others have argued that socialism did not *suppress* these identifications but *reinforced* them in specific ways.[43] They remain prominent in the postsocialist period, as groups seek to reorganize their interrelations following the demise of their putative identities as "socialist men," now superseded by "anticommunist" as a basic political identifica-tion. Sharp conflict around national identities has arisen above all from the dissolution of the Yugoslav and Soviet federations, as new nation-states

take their place. Conflicts to (re)define national identities implicate contests over time and space, for statues and revised histories often celebrate
specific sites and dates *as national*.

I find it helpful to assimilate national identities into the larger category of
social relations within which I think they belong: kinship. In my view, the
identities produced in nation-building processes do not displace those based
in kinship but—as any inspection of national rhetorics will confirm—rein-
force and are parasitic upon them. National ideologies are saturated with
kinship metaphors: fatherland and motherland, sons of the nation and their
brothers, mothers of these worthy sons, and occasionally daughters. Many
national ideologies present their nations as large, mostly patrilineal kinship
(descent) groups that celebrate founders, great politicians, and cultural figures as not just heroes but veritable "progenitors," forefathers—that is, as
ancestors. Think of George Washington, "Father of His Country," and
Atatürk, "Father Turk." (I say "patrilineal" because, as numerous scholars
have observed, nearly all the "ancestors" recognized in national ideologies
are male.[44])

Nationalism is thus a kind of ancestor worship, a system of patrilineal
kinship, in which national heroes occupy the place of clan elders in defining a nation as a noble lineage. This view is not original with me. It
appears in the work of anthropologists Edmund Leach, David Schneider,
and Meyer Fortes,[45] and in Benedict Anderson's suggestion that we treat
nationalism "as if it belonged with 'kinship' and 'religion,' rather than
with 'liberalism' or 'fascism.' "[46] Given this view, the work of contesting
national histories and repositioning temporal landmarks implies far more
than merely "restoring truth": it challenges the entire national genealogy.
This happens quite visibly in reburying a dead body, an act that inserts the
dead person differently as an ancestor (more central or more peripheral)
within the lineage of honored forebears. My focus on corpses enables me
to push this argument even further and to speak of the proper burials of
ancestors, which include revering them as cultural treasures.

ANCESTORS AND PROPER BURIAL   Any human community consists
not only of those now living in it but also, potentially, of both ancestors and
anticipated descendants. In a wry statement by a Montenegrin poet we see
part of this nicely: "We Montenegrins are a small population even if you

count our dead." Different human groupings place different emphases on these three segments of possible community—dead, living, and yet-unborn. Imperial China, for example, is renowned for having made ancestors into real actors in the world of the living, while in other societies ancestors are crucial points of reference for the living but inhabit their own world (though they may enter ours on occasion). Pro-natalist nationalist ideologies, by contrast, are preoccupied with *descendants*, connected to ancestors in an endless chain through time.

In many human communities, to set up right relations between living human communities and their ancestors depends critically on proper burial.[47] Because the living not only mourn their dead but also fear them as sources of possible harm, special efforts are made to propitiate them by burying them properly. The literature of anthropology contains many examples of burial practices designed to set relations with dead ancestors on the right path, so that the human community—which includes both dead and living—will be in harmony. Gillian Feeley-Harnik writes of such ancestor practices in Madagascar: "Ancestors are made from remembering them. Remembering creates a difference between the deadliness of corpses and the fruitfulness of ancestors. The ancestors respond by blessing their descendants with fertility and prosperity."[48] Their harmonious coexistence is about more than just getting along: it is part of an entire cosmology, part of maintaining order in the universe.

All human groups have ideas and practices concerning what constitutes a "good death," how dead people should be treated, and what will happen if they are not properly cared for. In what direction should the feet of the corpse be pointed? Who should wash it, and how should it be dressed? Can one say the name of the deceased person or not? How much time should elapse before burial? Is alcohol allowed at the wake? May the body be cremated without killing the person's chances for resurrection? What things must be said at the funeral? What kinds of gifts should be exchanged, and with whom? If one of these things is not done correctly, what will happen? Proper burials have myriad rules and requirements, and these are of great moment, for they affect the relations of both living and dead to the universe that all inhabit. Southern, Central, and Eastern Europe offer many examples of such conceptual worlds.[49] Although specific beliefs and practices vary widely across the region, for illustrative purposes they display sufficient commonalities to be treated together.

What goes into a proper burial? Kligman, Lampland, and Rév report[50] from contemporary Transylvanian and Hungarian ethnography that villagers there believe the soul of the deceased person watches the funeral, and if it is dissatisfied, it will return and punish the living by creating havoc, often in the form of illness. Was enough money thrown into the coffin? Were the burial clothes fine and comfortable? Was the deceased's favorite pipe put into the casket? If the person died unmarried, was a wedding also performed at his funeral? Various parts of the funeral ritual (the orientation of the body as it leaves the house, the reciprocal asking of forgiveness between living and dead, etc.) aim specifically to prevent a disgruntled soul from coming back. The possibilities for mayhem are much graver if the deceased had no burial at all.

In addition, for months and years after the funeral these villagers offer regular prayers and ritual meals to propitiate the dead and keep them quiet, believing that a well-fed, contented soul will protect its earthly kin.[51] One still finds ritual practices of this kind, for instance, in Transylvania and the former Yugoslavia. Every year a week after Easter, villagers go to the graves of kin in the cemetery, bearing special food cooked for the occasion; they sit on the graves and eat, offering the food to their dead.[52] For these people it is not enough that the dead be properly buried: the living must keep feeding their dead kin so as to ensure the ancestors' blessing and continued goodwill, which are essential to a well-ordered universe.[53]

From research in the Polish/Ukrainian borderland, Oltenia (Romania), and elsewhere we learn that a dead person who does not receive a proper burial has a number of options.[54] He may become a "walking dead man," annoy his family members, try to sleep with his wife, and seek to inflict retribution on those who wronged him. Or he may become a vampire. (These job choices are the preserve chiefly of males; unhappy dead females take on other forms.) One way or another, he makes the lives of his earthly relatives and neighbors unpleasant; they must either give him a proper burial (if he had none) or (if already buried) dig him up and cut off his head or drive a stake through his heart. Concern for the well-being of ancestors and other dead is thus crucial to peaceful living and to an orderly universe; proper burial helps to ensure these.

The idea that properly treated ancestors become protective spirits (or even saints) is found from Russia westward into Hungary, as is fear that a vengeful spirit will torment the living unless suitably placated. Such notions easily acquire deeper religious significance. Tumarkin describes, for instance, the link between the souls of ancestors and saints: in a Russian peasant house, icons often hang opposite the hearth, where the ancestors' souls are thought to reside. Russian Christianity absorbed forms of ancestor worship, which became an important part of cults of the saints; indeed, Russian peasants have long understood saints to be their adored forefathers who sacrificed themselves for future generations. "To light a candle for the saints," Tumarkin observes, "was to enter into spiritual discourse with the protective spirits of the past."[55]

Ideas about proper burial figure even in present-day dead-body politics. An example is the debates around whether to remove Lenin's mummy from its mausoleum in Moscow's Red Square. Like the corpse of Imre Nagy, Lenin's has been the object of much politicking. Although the idea of removing him and burying him somewhere else[56] is not new, starting in 1989 it was proposed and debated with increasing vigor. (The debate was briefly sidetracked by a report in *Forbes* magazine, also carried on U.S. TV programs such as ABC's *Evening News*, that Lenin was to be sold for hard currency at international auction.[57]) Having initially opposed the idea, Yeltsin later changed his mind, suggesting in 1993 and again in 1997 that Lenin be removed from Red Square for burial.[58] Then came the attacks on the statues of Tsar Nicholas and Peter the Great, fatal in the former instance; both were motivated, as I said, by opposition to Lenin's burial. The Russian Orthodox Church came out on the side of burying Lenin but refrained from stating whether the church would bury him as a "Christian." Meanwhile, the Duma voted to denounce the project for his removal, and the question of who (Yeltsin by presidential decree, the Federal Assembly, or the people by referendum) should make the final decision was tossed around like a hot potato. A poll taken in June 1997 showed clearly who favored burial and who did not: 54 percent supported the idea, and 32 percent opposed it; the latter were concentrated among supporters of Communist Party leader Gennady Zyuganov and some nationalists.[59]

One could say a great deal more on the politics behind Lenin's mummy (as does Vladislav Todorov, in a lengthy and often hilarious discussion[60]).

Market forces also have their effect. The embalmers who own the secret formula for Lenin reportedly took on after-hours work, catering to the fashions of newly wealthy Russians wanting to be embalmed; this moonlighting gives them another source of income, now that state funds for tending Lenin's mummy have dried up, and subsidizes their continuing to work on him.[61] But also important to determining Lenin's fate are ideas about what makes for a proper burial. Their relevance comes from the decidedly religious underpinnings of the Lenin cult, and from notions about the divine origin of the authority of the tsars (to whom Lenin was often compared).[62]

An embalmed and not-buried Lenin offends Russian Orthodox sensibility, according to which *every* dead person should be interred, with very specific rites.[63] For Russians, as for others discussed above, if someone is not buried or is buried improperly (or if *ab*normal people are given a "normal" burial), then bad things will happen.[64] Because an unburied body is a source of things not being quite right in the cosmos, this is in itself sufficient reason to place Lenin firmly in the soil. But the debate is complicated by another set of beliefs, one having to do with saints. In Russian Orthodox doctrine, a dead person is revealed to be a saint not only through miracles but also because the corpse does not putrefy. As is true in many parts of the world,[65] it used to be common Orthodox practice to exhume the dead after a certain time (three, five, or seven years was customary), wash the bones, and rebury them with a special liturgy. This ritual is still performed in some areas, including rural Greece.[66] If upon digging up a Russian corpse one found that it had not decayed, its preservation was a clear sign of sainthood.[67] Even though the incorruptibility of Lenin's corpse is a *human* achievement, he is still touched by these associations: dead people whose bodies have not decayed are holy.[68]

From the religious point of view, then, one can see that Lenin's mummy should be buried, lest bad things happen, and at the same time that it should *not* be buried but be exposed under glass, as befits a saint. In either case, the rationale has not just religious backing but roots in ideas about ongoing relations between the living and their dead. The only group excluded from arguments of this kind is the Communist Party, but it has ingeniously exploited other aspects of popular belief. In the parliamentary debate over what to do with Lenin, one of the communist participants reminded his audience that in 1941 Russian archaeologists had dug up the body of Tamerlane, about whom it was said that anyone who disturbed his grave would be cursed. Shortly thereafter, the Nazis overran the Soviet Union. The deputy concluded by asking what might happen if they now disturbed Lenin's casket to bury him![69] All these different and contradictory views about reburial are available for use in a political contest that I believe is enriched by including them, to enchant the kind of political analysis we might do on Lenin's corpse.[70]

I should clarify my aims in making these points about "proper burial": I both am and am not making an argument about the continuity of older beliefs and practices. Given that years of official atheism and relentless modernization have eroded many beliefs recorded in earlier ethnographic work, I would be foolish to presume continuity. Nonetheless, as Gail Kligman's wonderful book *The Wedding of the Dead* shows clearly for northern Romania in the 1970s, popular ideas such as those I have described were not erased during the socialist period.[71] Even Moscow intellectuals who think themselves beyond such "superstitions" can feel that there is something uncomfortably out of order about Lenin's unburied corpse.[72] But we should think about these seeming continuities carefully. Some practices that appear to be constant may actually have changed: for example, Andreesco and Bacou describe the modifications that distinguish burial practices in Oltenia (southern Romania) today from those of decades ago.[73] Assuming the trappings of modernity may mean that people no longer *feed* their ancestors, but they may still think it important to *recognize* them.

More important, however, is that some "traditional" practices are in fact reinforced (if not, indeed, invented, in Hobsbawm and Ranger's famous formulation[74]) by their present setting. Andreesco and Bacou indicate that far from suppressing older burial practices, Romanian socialism amplified some of them.[75] One reason might be that because religious burial violated official atheism, to bury one's dead properly was a form of resistance to official religious policy. A similar point emerges from a 1991 article in the *New York Times*, which reported that in Serbia as of the 1970s, practices involving hospitality and feasting in connection with the dead *increased*, as villagers began building entire houses on the graves of their relatives. These often lavish structures, with a coffin in the basement and regular feasting above, "so the spirit of the deceased has something to eat and drink," had less to do with tradition than with competitive displays among neighbors and against the Party elite.[76]

Thus, by invoking older beliefs and practices, I am not affirming unbroken continuity; the practices may be rejuvenated, attenuated, or simply invoked in discourse. What is most important about them is that those changes or invocations refer to practices that *have a history* (or histories). That history makes available numerous associations derived from earlier, precommunist times, forming a broader cultural system that shapes the possibilities for present political action. Political transformation may give "traditional" ideas new urgency—for example, proper burial and harmonious relations among kin may be especially powerful politically for those living through postsocialist times that have wrought such havoc on social relations among kinsmen, owing to conflicts over property restitution (which implicates kin above all others[77]). Ideas about proper burial, then, even if no longer held in a form identical to ideas from the past, enter into the penumbra of meanings that politicians and others can draw upon, alter, and intensify. These ideas and practices thereby inflect what can be done with dead-body symbolism.[78] The great stability of mortuary practices, mentioned earlier, lends further credence to this claim.

PROPER BURIAL AND CULTURAL TREASURES   I have one final point to make about proper burial. The point is specific to the cases of famous dead, such as Bartók, the heart of Bulgaria's Tsar Boris, and Romanian bishop Inochentie Micu (see chapter 2), who have returned from abroad. And I believe it applies to such cases not just in Eastern Europe but elsewhere as well. Even when ideas about vampires and the undead have gone out of style, one common rule about proper burial still in force is that *our "sons" must be buried on "our" soil*, lest we be plagued by misfortune arising from the soul's continued distress. The notion of repossessing "our" dead is common worldwide, as is evident from customs of warfare that return dead soldiers to their home countries. (Think of the ongoing preoccupation, in U.S. politics, with MIAs from the Korean and Vietnamese wars.) In such cases reburial at home may be presented simply as a matter of proper rest for the deceased, the idea that it prevents misfortune remaining at best implicit. We see this with a home-bound skeleton of a very different sort, that of the Sioux chief Long Wolf, brought back in September 1997 from London (where he had been "stranded" for 100 years) to his ancestral burial grounds in South Dakota. One of the Sioux who traveled to London to retrieve him observed after the funeral, "It means he's set free. He'll be among his own people. His bones will remain with us. The spirit remains with the bones, and the bones will finally be at rest among his own."[79]

What interests me in cases like this one and similar postsocialist examples is their perhaps unexpected link with national identities, the subject with which I began this section. That link is through the contemporary vogue, worldwide, for the return of cultural property or "heritage," an increasingly important part of building modern national identities. Over recent decades we have grown accustomed to peoples and countries, especially former colonies, petitioning to retrieve items of their cultural heritage or patrimony, often held by former colonial powers. Even Winnie-the-Pooh, Piglet, et al. have entered into the corpus of contested objects.[80] Efforts to define or redefine national identities seem increasingly to involve the notion that the "health" of a people is greatest when it has all its valued things at hand, rather than lying in museums or improper graves elsewhere. Perhaps the cases best known to residents of the United States involve the repatriation of Native American heritage—meaning both sacred objects and ancestral bones. The very word "repatriation" is eloquent: valued objects and remains are returning to the father- or homeland, where they should be.

In her fascinating book *The Return of Cultural Treasures*, Jeanette Greenfield observes that in the nineteenth century, cultural property of many kinds was "centralized," brought from its places of origin into museums in the major colonial centers.[81] We are now witnessing the opposite movement, as more and more museums are forced or volunteer to return their treasures to the places whence these were taken. Not every relic or object that moves is part of this aspect of postcolonialism, and not all bodies and objects are equally worth retrieving. The ones that are, however, are usually the bodies of persons thought to have contributed something special to their national history or culture. Adapting Greenfield, I would call them "cultural treasures." In many parts of the world it seems to have become very important to bring "our" treasures—whether they are valued objects or physical remains—back home where they "belong." The imagery of possession so often used inclines me to assimilate them to a worldwide concern with property rights—in this case, rights to *cultural* property.

This argument suggests that repatriating dead bodies in the postsocialist period is part of refurbishing (and fighting over) national identities by bringing "our cultural treasures" home for a proper burial—a burial that binds people to their national territories in an orderly universe.[82] These repatriations refurbish national identities by "nationalizing" symbolic capital that had entered global circuits, thus affirming the individuality of East European nation-states too long seen from without as barely distinguishable clones of international Soviet-style communism. Where the repatriates are world-famous, they may bring world respect, countering the arrogance of foreigners inclined to say, for instance, "Who would have thought that Romania, of all places, could produce cultural geniuses like Ionesco, Enescu, Eliade, and Brâncuşi!" This outcome is especially likely where the dead person himself has requested the homecoming (usually in a will), as is true of a number of the repatriated corpses. Perhaps the more respectable image they bring thereby will help their countries to be judged "European" and, thus, worthy of EU membership.

No matter whence the impetus for repatriations—from families of the deceased wanting royalties (as with Bartók; see introduction, note 37), from wills, or from governing parties hoping to consolidate a reputation as guardians of the national heritage—they draw wider notice and enhance the nation's global image. It is as if repatriating these cultural treasures and giving them proper burial localizes part of the symbolic capital they contain, just as postsocialist economies seek to attach themselves to international circuits in ways that will enable them to hold onto some of the profits for themselves. As I suggested at the beginning of this chapter, the corporeality of dead bodies facilitates such localizing claims. Their reburial participates in reordering meaningful worlds that are simultaneously conceptual, political, and economic.

• • •

In 1989, the ordering principles of daily life and the basic rules of the game in Soviet-bloc politics ceased to hold. The result was a high level of political conflict and disagreement as newly forming groups with vulnerable constituencies jockeyed for advantage in new political fields. An always fragile balance of political forces now underwent a profound shift, a shift so momentous that it warranted truly cosmic imagery and raised all manner of culturally deep concerns. What is the order of our world now that the Communist Party has fallen? Whom do we wish to recognize as our ancestors, now that Marx, Lenin, and local communists are out, and what genealogies do we wish to rewrite? How should we position ourselves relative to other people—who, that is, are our kin and trusted associates? How can we reset our moral compass? Who is to blame for what has happened, and how should they be punished?

Trying to resolve questions of this kind is what it means to reorder meaningful worlds. I have emphasized here the following aspects of that process: endowing postsocialist politics with a sense of the sacred, working toward a new moral order, assessing blame and seeking compensation, resignifying spatial and temporal landmarks and international borders, seeking modes of national self-affirmation and of connection with ancestors. Given all this, I think it is not too much to speak of reordering worlds of meaning as what is at stake in reburying the dead.

CONCLUSION

Let me recapitulate the arguments I have been making. My aims in the book as a whole are the descriptive one of presenting some material about the political "lives" of dead bodies in Eastern Europe and the former Soviet Union, and the analytical one of showing how we might think about that material within an enchanted, enlivened sense of politics. I see dead bodies as one of many vehicles through which people in postsocialist societies reconfigure their worlds of meaning in the wake of what I (and, I believe, they) regard as a profoundly disorienting change in their surroundings. The widespread disorientation offered tremendous opportunity to people seeking power, as well; the challenge for them was to form new political arenas, invent new rules of the game, and build new political identifications, all in fierce competition with other would-be elites. None of these outcomes, however, could simply be imposed. Only an alchemy mixing new political strategies with meanings already available would produce alternative political arrangements. I have suggested that the meanings already available included ideas about kinship, history, proper burial, and national identity; about authority, morality, space, and time. All these are important sites of new meaning-creation, by means of which political opportunists and disoriented citizens alike strive to reorder their meaningful worlds; moreover, dead bodies connect with all of them.

Not every theme I have raised is relevant to every politicized corpse: different themes illuminate different cases, as I try to show in my handling of the cases I discuss in chapters 2 and 3. There is no uniform interpretation of the political lives of dead bodies. My aim in this chapter has been to suggest a variety of ways for thinking about dead-body politics, to offer a loose framework for approaching examples whose details vary. Only sometimes will we clarify the meaning of one or another case through ideas about proper burial, for example, or through looking at the multiple résumés of their lives, as in the case of Nagy. Many things make Nagy's case unique in comparison with other reburials.[83] To understand any given case, one *might* find it helpful to ask what in present and past contexts gives what multiplicity of meanings to the résumé of that particular corpse: *How* does his complex biography make him a good instrument for revising history? What in his manifold activities encourages identification from a variety of people? Answering such questions will often, but not always, elucidate why some dead bodies rather than others become useful political symbols in transitional moments.

Why, you might inquire, do I go to such lengths to interpret dead bodies? Why isn't it sufficient to see them simply as part of legitimating postsocialist polities?[84] What is the payoff of all my talk about "meaningful worlds" and ancestor worship and burial practices, especially given my reluctance to see such practices as having continuity throughout communist rule? I believe I am in part discussing processes of legitimation, attempting to state more precisely what goes into them. But many of the reburials I discuss were initiated not by political leaders eager to establish new legitimacies but by humbler people hoping to rectify their worlds. Moreover, to label an event "legitimating" does not end the inquiry; it invites us to ask *how* that event legitimates *what*, and at whose initiative. In trying to explain why and how dead bodies work in postsocialist politics, I have presented legitimation as a process that employs symbols; in speaking of dead bodies as unusually ambiguous, protean symbols, I have pointed to the multiple possibilities lodged in a given corpse-qua-symbol that make it unusually effective in politics; and in discussing ancestors and burial rites, I have stressed that these symbols have histories, often deep ones, that further multiply the associations they provide as resources for creating meaning and legitimacy in moments of political contention. Thus my argument throughout this book concerns how we might think of legitimation in less rationalistic and more suitably "cosmic" terms, showing it as rich, complex, and disputatious processes of political meaning-creation—that is, as politics animated.

Is anything in these processes specific to the postsocialist context, distinguishing its many instances from uses of dead bodies elsewhere? I see three ways of answering this question in the affirmative. First, although corpses can be effective political symbols anywhere, they are pressed into the service of political issues specific to a given polity. For postsocialism, this means issues such as property restitution, political pluralization, religious renewal, and national conflicts tied to building nation-states. Such issues are found in other contexts, too, but in most postsocialist ones they occur simultaneously. This is an obvious argument for the specificity of postsocialist dead bodies, but not a strong one. Second, dead bodies— inherently yoking past with present—are especially useful and effective symbols for revising the past. To be sure, political transformation often involves such revision: indeed, communist parties revised pasts extensively. In Eastern Europe, however, rewriting history has been perhaps unusually necessary because of powerful pressures to create political identities based expressly on *rejecting* the immediate past. The pressures came not just from popular revulsion with communism but also from desires to persuade Western audiences to contribute the aid and investment essential to reconstruction. The revisionist histories that corpses and bones embodied were therefore central to *dramatizing* the end of Communist Party rule.

Finally, I believe dead bodies are uncommonly lively in the former socialist bloc because of the vastness of the transformations there that make bodies worth fighting over, annexing, and resignifying. The specificity of postsocialist corpses lies in the magnitude of the change that has animated them. The *axis mundi* has shifted; whole fields of the past await the plowshare of revisionist pens, as well as the tears of those whose dead lie there insufficiently mourned. A change so momentous and far-reaching requires especially heavy, effective symbols, symbols such as dead bodies. I am suggesting, then, that the specificity of postsocialist dead-body politics, compared with examples from elsewhere, is a matter not of kind but of degree.

The remaining two chapters treat specific cases with the tools I think best suited to them from those I have mentioned. The two chapters are organized very differently: one in the manner of a chronological narrative and the other more like a network of ideas that double back on themselves; the differences in organization are part of the message I hope to convey by the end of the book. In both chapters I strive to bring in the delights of anthropology, too often ignored in the literature on postsocialism: a respect for wide variability on a small scale; close attention to how these particulars intersect with contemporary global processes—how everyday and large-scale forces intersect in particular skeletons in the wake of communism's collapse; and ideas about ancestors, about "proper burial," about the cosmos, morality, and blame, about time and space, and about death and rebirth. I hope the result will demonstrate how we might enchant our sense of the political and enliven our understanding of politics in the postsocialist world.

I will have more to say when I am dead.

—EDWIN ARLINGTON ROBINSON

CHAPTER TWO

The Restless Bones of Bishop Inochentie Micu

- 18ᵗʰ century

Emphasizing action of reli Elites

-Buried in Romania after got returned Aron Bre
1997

*H*aving offered in the introduction and chapter 1 two kinds of
surveys—one of postsocialist dead bodies, and one of concepts for thinking about them—it is time for more extended illustration than I have given
so far. Chapters 2 and 3 illustrate, using different but overlapping analytic
strategies, how we might interpret the political lives of some dead bodies.
In this chapter I describe the politicking in Romania around a single
famous set of bones, emphasizing the actions of religious elites; in the
next, I focus on multiple "nameless" skeletons and corpses as these entered
into both nationalist politics and the feelings and beliefs of ordinary folk
in the former Yugoslavia.

My moving skeleton on this occasion is Bishop Inochentie Micu,[1] an
eighteenth-century Transylvanian clergyman who returned from Rome
to Romania in August 1997 and was reburied there in October of that year.

+ Roman Othodox Church-as "monopoly"

It was a major happening—for a small number of people. Although many
Romanians had heard of Micu (from their school history books), few were
aware of the disputes over his reburial.[2] The event received little media
coverage, nor was the service in October broadcast live, as might have
been appropriate. My idle conversations with people other than clergymen
or lay activists turned up very few who knew what was going on around
Micu. Indeed, one of my interviewees justified in these words the lengthy
afternoon that he accorded our conversation: "We need publicity, and
you're going to give it to us!" (Several people on the opposite side, by contrast, urged me not to blow the controversy out of proportion or even give
it much thought.[3])

Therefore I claim neither that Inochentie Micu's reburial provoked
much consciousness-raising or "world-reordering" among the general
public, nor that the disputes focused widespread societal energies (they
were mainly a priestly and intellectual preoccupation). Micu is interesting
not in the way of Lenin, the tsar, or Imre Nagy, but because of the unexpected facets of postsocialist transformation that comprehending his
body's political life challenges us to take up, facets that are world-reordering indeed. They include property restitution, wholesale reassessments of
national history and identity, and a global rivalry among religious faiths.
It is the convergence of these forces, I believe, that set his bones in motion.
Grasping the links between his highly local significance(s) and a worldwide reorganization of religions makes him a case study in the interaction
of local and global processes.

The story of Inochentie's reinterment embraces nearly all the themes I
raised in chapter 1. It was an effort to reorganize social relations and property ownership between persons and religious communities. It proposed a
substantial revision of Romanians' national genealogy and new values for
the temporal landmarks of Romanian history. It was charged with questions about moral authority, accountability, compensation, and the moral
values to which a postsocialist Romania should hold. It underscored a
clash between two competing alternatives for how to sacralize political
authority: by making one particular church (Romanian Orthodox) an official "monopoly" church of the state or by insisting on plural faiths, each
with its own civil guarantees, all sacralizing authority jointly through an
emphasis on faith as central to Romanian identity. In addition, the episode

- marks the end of official Atheism in Romania

mobilized intense feeling, partly because of his biography and some interesting ambiguities in his "résumé" (that is, his multivocality as a politico-
religious symbol), a point I illustrated earlier with Imre Nagy.

I have chosen not to organize my analysis of Inochentie's political life
explicitly around the concept of reordering that underlies all these themes,
however, for I think the particulars of the case stand out better with a different narrative organization. Instead, I begin with his local specifics and
progress upward to the global context without which his bones might not
have sprung to life. In brief, here is my argument. I approach Inochentie
Micu's restless bones with the following questions: Why, some 229 years
after he died, did he leave Rome and travel to a second, more fulsome burial in the Transylvanian town of Blaj? Why *now*, when the idea of his repatriation is more than two centuries old? What passions and intrigues
intersect in his corpse? Why should we take note?

Idea

To answer them, I begin with his actual person in its time and proceed
first to the post-1989 struggle for property and believers among churches in
Romania, then to the global religious reorganization sparked by the end of
official atheism in the former Soviet bloc. The fall of Communist Party
rule opened a tremendous field for renewing religious belief and, at the
same time, an unprecedented competition for believers. These changes
occurred as part of shifts in interfaith relations on a world scale—from the
rise of Islamic fundamentalism challenging other forms of Islam, to the
new influence of the Christian right in U.S. politics, to the attempts at ecumenism involving the Roman Catholic, Greek Orthodox, and various
Protestant churches. Particularly in the former Soviet Union, some eighty
million Russian Orthodox Christians exposed to over seventy years of official atheism and perfunctory liturgies from a church subservient to the
Communist Party might be thought ripe for conversion to some other
faith. Not only did Protestant missionaries head eastward by the plane-
load;[4] high-stakes maneuvering also developed among leaders of the
Russian and Constantinople (Istanbul) Orthodox churches and the Roman
Catholic Church. Islam figures also, for some of these men have sought
alliances with or against it as part of their contest. (The same shift in interfaith relations appeared in Bosnia, as Roman Catholic Croats and Bosnian
Muslims allied against Orthodox Serbs.)

I cannot tell the whole story of Inochentie Micu's perambulations, just

Fall of Communist - remarks., renewing
religious beli

enough to sketch the links among an eighteenth-century cleric, postsocialism, Pope John Paul II, and Russia's Patriarch Alexei II.[5] By means of political corpses and using an approach at once ethnographic and macrosocial, I throw perhaps unexpected light on how socialism is being transformed.

WHO WAS BISHOP INOCHENTIE MICU?

There is no better place to start than with Inochentie of the restless bones himself. Who was he? Let's open two windows on our computer screen. On one is the crypt of the Madonna del Pascolo Church in Rome (now the Rome offices of the Ukrainian Greek Catholic Church). Inside we see a stone sarcophagus with Inochentie's name carved into it;[6] his bones rested there from his death in 1768 until July 1997. On our second window we see a copy of his testament, sent in 1756 from Rome to the Greek Catholic bishop in Blaj, Transylvania, and housed in the library of the theological school Inochentie had founded in that town. We read:

> I know not what sweetness attracts us to our natal soil and keeps us from forgetting it. My days are waning; when my soul must leave my body, I would like it to be entrusted to the Creator by your prayers and offices, and my bones to await the universal resurrection in your monastery at Blaj.[7]

We see, then, that he asked to come home quite a while ago. But who *is* this fellow? Answering that question requires knowing something about eighteenth-century Transylvania and also about an institution many readers will find unfamiliar: the Catholic Church of the Byzantine Rite, or the Church United with Rome, or (as I will call it) the Greek Catholic Church.[*]

That institution, in turn, is part of a centuries-long three-way struggle among the Ottoman, Romanov (or Russian), and Habsburg empires for mastery of the space now called Eastern Europe. Although the Ottomans

---

[*] This church is also known as the Uniate Church, a term I avoid because of its somewhat pejorative meaning for people of that faith. To avoid confusion, I will employ the term "Catholic" in this chapter whenever the difference between Roman and Greek Catholicism is unimportant, and will otherwise qualify "Catholic" with one adjective or the other.

- Each empire helds diff. religions → struggles

- Battle in Transylvania & Ukraine[59]

held the initial advantage following their capture of Constantinople in 1453, by the 1680s the balance was reversed. Each empire had its dominant religion—respectively, Islam, Eastern Orthodoxy, and Roman Catholicism (itself at war against the Protestant Reformation)—and religion was prominent in their struggles. The intra-Christian (Catholic-Orthodox) rivalry was intense, particularly once Ottoman power faded, leaving as the two main contenders Habsburgs and Romanovs, Catholicism and Orthodoxy. As the two empires strove to expand their frontiers into one another's territory, the principal battlefield lay across Transylvania and western Ukraine.

Imperial dynasts fought not only with each other but also with other social groups who resisted their expanding power; chief among these were the landed nobility, who felt imperial centralization as a blow to themselves. Although this struggle took place throughout all the empires, it was unusually complex in Transylvania, which the Habsburgs were then trying to absorb. Having enjoyed quasi-autonomous status within the Ottoman empire for 175 years,[8] Transylvania acceded to the Habsburg realm not by conquest but by the consent of the province's noble Parliament (or Diet). This left intact both the nobles' political base and a very complicated social structure, with a confusing mix of languages, privileged feudal estates and unprivileged serfs, and official and unofficial religions. The following points are essential for Inochentie Micu's story:

1. The three main language groups were what we now call Hungarian, German, and Romanian.

2. Three groups made up the *populus,* or privileged feudal estates (called *nationes,* or "nations"—though not yet in the ethnic sense[9]). These were known as nobles, Szeklers, and Saxons; the first two spoke forms of the Hungarian language, and the third, a form of German. Among the privileged *nationes* were almost no native speakers of Romanian, who formed the bulk of the serf population, or *plebs.* Each of the *nationes* was associated with a territory, whereas (Romanian-speaking) serfs lived interspersed on the territories of the other three. There were also some free peasants, largely Romanian-speakers and located largely on the Saxon territories. (Inochentie Micu's family was of this type.)

3. The different social and linguistic groups had different religions. As of the Reformation, Transylvania had four "accepted" (privileged) religions: Lutheranism (Saxons), Roman Catholicism (usually the wealthier Hungarian nobles), and Calvinism and Unitarianism (many Hungarian nobles and Szeklers). Because of the concord among them, sixteenth-century Transylvania was Europe's center of religious toleration, to which people fled from religious persecution in places like England. There was also a fifth religion, Eastern Orthodoxy, practiced by Romanian-speaking serfs and free peasants; it did not hold the privileged status of the other four and was merely a "tolerated" religion. Its priests, in contrast to other clergy, were mostly serfs, like their flock. In Transylvania's layer cake of languages, occupations, wealth, and religion, Protestants were the most influential politically, Catholics were generally the wealthiest, and Eastern Orthodox Romanian-speakers were at the bottom on all counts. (This simplifies the situation, but not by much; see table 1.)

TABLE 1. Social Structure in Eighteenth-Century Transylvania

Language Group	Religion		Feudal Estate (Name)	
Hungarian	Roman Catholic		Nobles	
	Calvinist	("Received" religions)	Szeklers	(*Populus*)
	Unitarian			
German	Lutheran		Saxons	
Romanian	Eastern Orthodox ("Tolerated")		Serfs (*Plebs*) Some free peasants* (mostly in Saxon lands)	

*Inochentie Micu's family was from this stratum.

For the Habsburgs, empire-building against both Russians and nobles had a strong religious element, giving the Reformation and Counter-Reformation there a distinctive color. Owing to Protestant dominance in Transylvania, the Habsburgs and their Jesuit advisers found themselves fighting religious wars on two fronts: against the Protestant nobles and against Russia's local protégés, the Orthodox serfs. The Habsburg Counter-Reformation in Transylvania aimed at converting both Protestant nobles and the vastly larger Orthodox population, reasoning that if the serfs became Habsburg allies (i.e., Catholics), that would further weaken the nobles' power. → Protestants

Transylvania's Protestants had been trying their own version of this tactic for over a century, engaging in a lengthy offensive to convert the Romanians to Protestantism. Toward this end they had printed the first Romanian-language Bibles and other religious books. In their case the aim was not empire-building but tying down their Romanian Orthodox labor force, which kept fleeing—unimpeded by major religious or linguistic differences—across the Carpathian Mountains into the Ottoman-dominated Romanian Principalities, where tribute and labor dues were less onerous than in Transylvania. Protestants had been proselytizing the Orthodox serfs for 150 years by the time the Habsburg Counter-Reformation began.

The Habsburgs, however, chose an instrument more suited to converting the serfs because it was closer to Orthodox doctrines and rituals than was Protestantism. The instrument was "Uniatism," which combined Roman Catholicism and Eastern Orthodoxy to produce the so-called Greek Catholic Church. Its liturgy and ritual would be those of Orthodoxy, but its doctrine would follow Roman Catholicism in recognizing the supremacy of the pope and in three particulars.[10] This idea was not new: Jesuits in the Polish court had successfully catholicized Orthodox peoples in Ruthenia and the Ukraine a century before by these same means, so the Uniatist concept had an important precedent.[11] Added to the religious incentives for conversion was the Habsburgs' promise that those Orthodox clergy who converted would gain the privileges of Catholic clergy—an appealing thought for Orthodox priests, treated as serfs and subject to heavy dues in labor and money. If Orthodox clergy could be persuaded to convert, reasoned the Jesuits, they would perforce bring their congregations with them.

Here, then, are the forces behind the tug-of-war that developed between the Transylvanian nobility and the Habsburg dynasts; the rope they used was the largely Orthodox and Romanian-speaking serf population, pulled this way and that. In the event, the Habsburgs were more successful. The higher clergy of the Orthodox Church in Transylvania accepted the Greek Catholic faith in a series of synods between 1697 and 1700. By 1733, according to their count, there were six times as many Greek Catholic priests as Orthodox.[12] Thus, the Romanian-speaking population of Transylvania was religiously divided in two: Orthodox and Greek Catholic. The next seven decades saw great upheaval, as some of the serfs refused to follow their priests into abandoning Orthodoxy.

Meanwhile, the Habsburgs dragged their feet on implementing the privileges promised to Greek Catholic priests. They proved unable to override the opposition of the Transylvanian nobility, which objected strenuously (and with good reason) to promises that emancipated not just clergy who became Greek Catholic, but also any serf who did so.[13] At most, the nobles granted Greek Catholic clergy a few minor privileges, such as free salt.

Life start

This was the context in which Inochentie's life takes on significance and his travels in 1997 have sense. Born Ioan Micu in 1692[14] to an Orthodox family, he was schooled by Jesuits (whom he had impressed with his intelligence), accepted into the Basilian monastic order (he took the name Inochentie then), and appointed Greek Catholic bishop of Transylvania in 1729, with the noble title of baron and a place in Transylvania's Diet. Even before he was officially installed, however, he began pressing the court in Vienna to fulfill the promise that Greek Catholic conversion would bring Catholic privileges and an end to serf status. Insisting on this first for clergy and other Greek Catholic converts, then for *all* Romanians, became a veritable campaign that he pursued tirelessly, through forty years of repeated petitions to the Habsburg court. He strengthened the Greek Catholic Church in hopes of using it to raise the Romanian *plebs* to the status of *natio*.[15] Ingeniously seizing upon (and furthering) the emergent ethnic sense of the feudal *natio*, he launched the Romanian national movement. His closely reasoned petitions became founding documents for the *Supplex Libellus Valachorum*, a brilliant manifesto written by Greek Catholics educated in the schools he had founded, which laid out the theoretical

Defense of Political Rights for Romanians

— Exile - of refusion

arguments in defense of political rights for Romanians.[16] Through his persistence he aroused the wrath both of Empress Maria Theresa and of the Transylvanian Diet, to whom emancipating the feudal labor force was unthinkable. Living in exile from 1744 on and compelled to abdicate his bishopric in 1751, he died in Rome in 1768.

Persons of both Greek Catholic and Orthodox faith regard Inochentie as a great national hero, and justly so. He displayed true genius in reworking the feudal idiom of *natio* in the service of his ethnic nation. According to Romania's preeminent historian, David Prodan (born Orthodox), Inochentie "unquestionably stand[s] out in Romanian history as the most powerful political personality of the Romanian people in eighteenth century Transylvania."[17] Even the Orthodox Church has shown its special regard for him, by putting out icons on which he is labeled an *Orthodox* bishop! Indeed, throughout the communist period (when Greek Catholics were unable to object) the Orthodox Church sought to condemn the Greek Catholic Church while making Inochentie theirs. According to Orthodox historiography, Greek Catholicism represents not the beginning of rights for Romanians but opportunistic priests' odious betrayal of Romanians' ancestral faith in exchange for some salt. Far from being a landmark in the Romanian national struggle, they say, Greek Catholicism sabotaged that struggle by dividing the Romanian nation between two faiths, one pure and ancestral, the other an abominable corruption from the West.[18]

Inochentie escapes this condemnation, however, for the Orthodox hierarchy has made him both a national hero and an Orthodox one. Against the Greek Catholic view that his exile resulted from his refusal to give up either the national struggle or his Greek Catholic faith, revisionist Orthodox hagiography attributes it to his supposed threat that unless the Habsburgs kept their promises, he would abandon Greek Catholicism and return with all his faithful to Orthodoxy. An Orthodox priest I spoke with put it thus: "Inochentie was a fighter for Romanian rights. He wasn't in the Greek Catholic Church for reasons of faith but was permanently tied to our traditional [i.e., Orthodox] beliefs." In other words, having opportunistically taken on the Greek Catholic faith to raise up his people, he was ready, like a true national hero, to return to the ancestral church when his reasons for converting failed. (Although that argument is not totally far-fetched, the evidence for it is very thin.[19])

16 Transylvania's Greek Catholic Bishop Ioan Inochentie Micu-Klein
(1692–1768).

With this summary of who he was, we might now pursue the question, Why did he return to Transylvania only in 1997, if people have known of his desire to do so since 1756? The beginnings of an answer are simple: round numbers. There is something about round numbers that seems to invite celebration, especially *big* round numbers like 2000, marking two millennia of Christendom. The Vatican approaches the year 2000 in a highly festive mood. It is the good fortune of Transylvania's Greek Catholics that this great round-number festivity incorporates a smaller one of their own: three hundred years since the Acts of Union establishing their church in 1697–1700. That happy coincidence immediately points to the possible instigators of Inochentie's move from Rome: Greek Catholics, using their three hundredth anniversary to honor the man who is undoubtedly the most worthy of their ancestors. By reburying Inochentie, they would publicize his (and their own) pivotal place *qua Greek Catholics* in Romanians' national genealogy. Such a move would substantially revise communist-era histories, raising to prominence a community that had nearly become extinct.

My conversations with both Greek Catholic and Orthodox laypeople and clergy indicated that Greek Catholics were indeed the source of the plan that brought Inochentie home to rest. Together with a few non-Greek Catholic politicians (including former President Ion Iliescu), Greek Catholic clergy and laypeople successfully sought permission from Pope John Paul II for removing his bones from Rome.[20] They thereby enabled Inochentie finally to set metatarsal on native soil, fulfilling both his testament and the longstanding idea of bringing him back.[21] But if round numbers are the answer, why wait until 300? Why was Inochentie brought home only *now*? Why do Greek Catholics need to reinsert themselves into the national genealogy precisely in the 1990s?

INOCHENTIE BEGINS TO STIR

A crucial detail is that after the Romanian communists took power in 1948, under the Soviet aegis, they banned the Greek Catholic Church—despite its 250 years as an active, independent force in Romanians' political and spiritual life—confiscated its property, and forcibly merged its followers with the Romanian Orthodox Church.[22] Among the motives were pressure from Moscow to unify all Orthodox churches in the region, making them sub-

servient to the Russian patriarch (who would be subservient to Stalin), and
to eliminate anything that might reduce Soviet influence. In particular, the
Greek Catholics' obedience to the pope—fully beyond Stalin's reach—
made them an alternative center of spiritual gravity that was intolerable.[23]
Romanian communists therefore jailed all Greek Catholic clergy and many
laypeople who refused the merger, including all six bishops and all six successor bishops whom they had ordained. Not one of the twelve Greek
Catholic bishops (and, following their example, few other Greek Catholic
clerics) gave in to the Party's tempting offers of high salaries and top jobs if
they would become Orthodox. Most of them died in prison, providing
today's Greek Catholics with martyrs and exemplars of intransigence to
hold up against the Romanian Orthodox Church, which compromised with
the communists. Many Greek Catholics became either Roman Catholics or
Orthodox (some of them pro forma); others took Greek Catholic religious
observance underground.

Competition Over Property

Soon after the change of regime in 1989, the 1948 decree merging the two
churches was abrogated and Greek Catholics reemerged into the light. They
did so quite literally, in fact, for in 1948 the use of their properties and church
buildings had gone to the Orthodox Church, which now proved reluctant to
give them back.[24] Some Greek Catholic congregations celebrated their
liturgy in the buildings of Roman Catholics, or occasionally in those of
benevolent Orthodox priests; in some communities the matter was peace-
fully resolved by turning over one of two Orthodox church buildings to the
Greek Catholics. But the 1990s saw numerous open-air Greek Catholic services as well, their celebrants unable to secure access to places of worship.[25]
With the Orthodox hierarchy vigorously opposing Greek Catholics' efforts
to retrieve churches they had once owned, there have been protracted conflicts over church property, especially buildings.[26] It is a very lopsided contest, given the sizes of the two contenders: Greek Catholics number about a
quarter-million (in a hotly disputed census); the at-least-nominally
Orthodox, about twenty million.[27] Nonetheless, the Greek Catholics have
great political and moral capital (their widely acknowledged role in producing Romanian national consciousness and emancipation, their moral claims

[handwritten annotations: "church's struggle for lost lands & territories in Transyvalnis; conflict Greek Catholics & Orthodox (Catholic)" / "Route"]

to compensation for their suffering under the communists), and this improves their chances—as do their ties with the Vatican, as we shall see.

Conflicts over church buildings participate in much larger struggles around property, as post-1989 governments throughout Eastern Europe grapple with the problem of what to do with "socialist property" of all kinds (whether "donated" to the state by former owners, confiscated, or produced by collective labor during the socialist period). Should confiscated and "donated" property be returned? If so, how? The matter has proved much more intractable than was at first imagined. Concerning Romania's church property in particular, conflicts involve Catholics, Calvinists, Unitarians, and Lutherans as well as Greek Catholics and Orthodox, for *all* churches lost land and buildings in 1948; the post-1989 trend toward property restitution gave them a chance at redress. Although I will restrict myself here to the Greek Catholic–Orthodox conflict that has animated Inochentie's bones, I mention the wider field of religious property claims, for they inevitably connect with national identity—and this, too, affects the Greek Catholic-Orthodox conflict.

Conflicts over buildings happen largely in Transylvania, with a few also arising in Bucharest. Within Transylvania, they occur in both urban and rural areas, although they differ by region. Rural incidents are especially common in the north (Maramureş), where the numbers of the two religions are more closely balanced than elsewhere; in general, however, because Greek Catholics are more likely to live in cities, more incidents are urban.[28] News reports as well as my interviewees describe events in which Orthodox villagers burn the houses of Greek Catholics, threaten their priests, and surround and beat them after blocking their way into church. In a television news broadcast in July 1997, for instance, villagers of both faiths hurled imprecations at each other, as the Orthodox side blared rock music at top volume over loudspeakers to drown out the service they had forced the Greek Catholics to hold outdoors. After the Orthodox clergy in one town agreed to transfer their church building to its former Greek Catholic owners, parishioners razed the church to the ground. In the Transylvanian city of Cluj, Greek Catholics unable to repossess their buildings held outdoor services in the square next to the Gothic-style Roman Catholic (Hungarian) cathedral (see plates 17–18), fueling Orthodox-inspired rumors that Greek Catholics are closet Hungarians and want to separate Transylvania from Romania.

[handwritten annotation: "Quot ?"]

17 Open-air Greek Catholic church service in Cluj, Romania, July 1997. The building in the background is the Roman Catholic cathedral; in the foreground is an archeological site of some Roman ruins being excavated by order of Cluj's Romanian nationalist Mayor, Gheorghe Funar, in hopes of finding Roman skeletons that might be Romanian ancestors.

18 Open-air Greek Catholic church service in Cluj, Romania.

When, in March 1998, a Romanian court ruled that the Orthodox Church must return the Schimbarea la Faţa church building that Greek Catholics claimed as their seat, fistfights broke out between adherents of the two faiths. Exactly a week later, Cluj Archbishop Anania, with the support of several other high clerics, organized a silent demonstration of some six thousand Orthodox priests and laypersons; the aim of the march, which ended at the Schimbarea la Faţa church, was to "pray for the enemies of Romania and of the Romanian Orthodox Church."[29]

In an effort to resolve the disputes over property, Greek Catholic priest/Senator Matei Boilă introduced into Romania's Parliament in mid-1997 a bill to regulate the return of formerly Greek Catholic church buildings.[30] The bill passed the lower house, then was stalled in committee for a long time; when it finally reached the upper house, it failed, and (as of summer 1998) was not reintroduced. Speculation in newspapers and among those with whom I spoke was that the Orthodox hierarchy had intervened to kill it, once they saw its passage was likely.[31] If true, this explanation would show how the Orthodox Church benefits from its size and its status as the unofficial "state" church to influence political solutions to the property question.

Another way in which the Orthodox Church resists Greek Catholic challenges to church buildings is by promoting a particular definition of property entitlement. Capitalizing upon the Communist Party's 1948 decree, which held that church properties belong not to the church as an *institution* but to the *faithful* (this enabled the Party to confiscate all properties belonging to "faithful" who had "disappeared," such as Greek Catholics), the Orthodox Church employs a definition of property entitlement very different from that of Catholics. For the latter, the buildings belong to the church as an institution: even if all believers quit, the church building still belongs to the Catholic Church. For the Orthodox hierarchy, by contrast, according to a 1993 treatise on canon law, the buildings belong collectively to the faithful; the more numerous the faithful, the more the buildings they should have.[32] It is easy to see why this argument would appeal to them in a time when a handful of Greek Catholics are challenging the much more numerous Orthodox believers for houses of worship.

Greek Catholics see the intransigence of the Orthodox Church on the *making church into monopoly " we gives you*

property question in precisely these materialist terms.[33] One priest I spoke with claimed to have asked Orthodox Archbishop Anania of Cluj point-blank why he was leading the resistance to the return of church buildings, and to have received the following answer: "Frankly, because if we give you churches, you'll take our believers." In conversation, a historian who is Orthodox summarized the issue concisely: "The whole church conflict is a question not of faith but of revenues; the more believers you have, the more dough you'll get." These economic arguments surely have merit, given that between 1990 and 1997 alone, the Orthodox Church began building 949 new Orthodox churches; another 977 churches are in urgent need of repair. Moreover, there are plans for a ten-thousand-place "Cathedral for our Nation's Salvation" (on the scale of the restored Cathedral of Christ Our Savior in Moscow), to be built on five hectares near Bucharest at a projected cost of one trillion lei.[34]

The plot, therefore, thickens. In summoning Inochentie to return, Greek Catholics are enlisting him in fights over property, so common to postsocialism, in which the Greek Catholic Church is embroiled to the hilt. The stakes of these fights include the very possibility of Greek Catholics' full religious revival. For them, bringing Inochentie home means forging an alliance with a great national hero (even the Orthodox Church says so) and gaining tremendous visibility through him. This is occurring at precisely the moment when the Orthodox Church, too, wants to consolidate its new freedom of religious practice, only to discover itself challenged for the buildings in which expanded worship might take place. (Also embroiled in such conflicts over church buildings are Orthodox and both Greek and Roman Catholics in Ukraine, another center of high religious ferment. The dissension there produced a totally different kind of dead-body politics; the coffin of a Greek Catholic archbishop sat for days on the sidewalk, occasioning huge demonstrations and masses of flowers, because various Orthodox and Greek Catholic factions could not agree on where to bury him.[35])

The strife between Greek Catholics and Orthodox concerning church property far outstrips Inochentie's reburial in importance. In describing this strife, I do not mean to suggest that Inochentie sits at the center of it. Since my subject is not church conflict but the politics of dead bodies, I

devote space to that conflict in order to reveal the politics around his
bones—which, in turn, tells us a great deal about the complexities of postsocialist transformation. Returning property is central to that transformation; one can find its effects in countless areas of life, of which interchurch
relations is one. But the property question is also part of a much larger
reordering—of ideas about morality and accountability, and of people's
social relations. How should reparation be made for socialism's breach of
property rights? Whose moral standards should define future conduct,
those of Greek Catholic priests and bishops, or those of the Orthodox—
and according to what evaluation of these? I believe that it is partly for
reordering moralities and the social relations of property that Greek
Catholics sought Inochentie's aid, and that Orthodox clerics so vigorously opposed them.

PROblem of Othodox

Troubles Within Romanian Orthodoxy

The "real-estate question" is pivotal for Greek Catholics because it is
urgent if they are to survive. The Orthodox Church, on the other hand,
faces difficulties of other kinds, having to do with its capacity to draw followers and retain those it has. Characteristically for Eastern Orthodox
churches, the Romanian one has long enjoyed a special relationship with
the Romanian state, even under Communist Party rule. Although the
Party placed serious constraints on church activities and compelled Party
members not to participate in them, it did not ban the church outright—in
fact, it paid priests a salary. Perhaps in exchange, the Orthodox Church not
only declined to oppose the Party but also collaborated with it. Many

Orthodox clergy served the regime as Secret Police informers—and some
have even admitted this publicly.[36] Since 1989 it has struggled to find its
feet, its reputation for craven subservience having compromised it in the
eyes of many parishioners. In short, Orthodoxy has a serious credibility
problem, and it must embark on renewal if it is to reengage the many
Romanians who fell away from it after 1948. Worsening the problem is
that forty years without serious religious education produced nominal
churchgoers who no longer know their own Orthodox religion. Bibles
were published in print runs of some five thousand,[37] and many of the best
priests were jailed, leaving the church to the weaker and less energetic.

Much of the church hierarchy is now elderly and unwilling to think about how to renew the institution and reinvigorate its members' faith.

For those who do, divisions have emerged as to how such renewal should be accomplished. Aged Patriarch Teoctist finds himself trying to balance between the church's "fundamentalists" of mystical and pro-Moscow orientation and its more secularized adherents. Further divisions come from differences of opinion among both clergy and Orthodox laypeople as to how to manage relations (particularly the property question) with the Greek Catholics.[38] As Teoctist approaches the end of his reign, a quiet struggle for the patriarch's seat has developed among the most powerful Romanian archbishops. Given that the last few patriarchs have moved to that post from the archdiocese of Iaşi, there seems to be a "tradition" that Iaşi makes the patriarch. Partly with this in mind, in 1990 a deal was struck within the church to retain the communist-era Teoctist as patriarch in exchange for his appointing to the Iaşi archdiocese a young reformist priest, Daniel, trained at Princeton and Geneva seminaries, who would succeed him. For various reasons, however, several of the clerics whose vote in the synod will be critical to electing a new patriarch are hesitant to back Daniel, opening up the possibility that an older archbishop might be named instead. The result has been very delicate maneuvering, as various archbishops stake out positions either more progressive and enlightened or more intransigently conservative than Daniel's.[39]

Daniel, meanwhile, has gained much visibility through yet another dead body, whom he invited to Romania for its first visit in nearly two millennia. The visitor was St. Andrew (in fact only his skull, which seems to be all there is), whom Romanians regard as their Christianizer and patron saint. Normally housed in a monastery at Patras, Greece, in October 1996 St. Andrew's skull traveled to Iaşi, arriving at the time of the annual public display of the eleventh-century relics of Saint Paraschiva.[40] With these two famous relics reinforcing one another, Iaşi and its enterprising archbishop suddenly gained much visibility. Even the main candidates in Romania's then upcoming presidential election presented themselves before these saints, so TV cameras could show them venerating two eminent icons of Romanian spirituality. After visiting two other Romanian cities, St. Andrew headed back (as it were) to Patras.

Competition Around Romanian Identity

It is this Orthodox Church, then, rife with internal disagreements, that at the prospect of Inochentie's return found itself in sharp conflict with the Greek Catholics whose leader he once was. Aside from property questions, another theme one uncovers both in church literature and in disagreements about proper burial for Inochentie is, Which church is more closely tied to Romanian national identity? From conversations and publications I encountered in asking about Inochentie, I found much to suggest two churches vying for special identification with "the Romanian people/nation." The rivalry occurs around several themes, some of them historical. One is, Which church contributed more to national consciousness? Romanian history books for decades have claimed that Inochentie and his Greek Catholic heirs inaugurated the political movement for Romanian rights,[41] and this view is widely held today by members of both faiths. In the communist period the Orthodox Church made its own claim to preeminence in the national history, namely, that shared Orthodox worship had enabled Romanians to survive centuries of foreign rule as a single nation, despite their division across three spheres of Habsburg, Russian, and Ottoman influence. These two views need not be mutually exclusive: each church contributed something important, one a political movement and one a shared identity. Carried further, however, these moderate positions become antagonistic. In the absence of contention over other things, the conciliatory view might prevail, as some in each church would like. But this is a contentious moment.

Another point of discord concerns which church has been with Romanians the longer. One of the basic weapons in Romanians' national arsenal against other groups in the area is that "the Romanian people was born Christian," for it arose from the mixture of Christianized Roman soldiers and colonists with the indigenous Dacians they defeated in 105–106 C.E. (Other national groups, by contrast, were Christianized much later— the Slavs by Cyril and Methodius in the ninth century, the Hungarians in the tenth.) During the communist period the distinction of longevity automatically went to the Romanian Orthodox Church, but with the Greek Catholic resurgence the question reappears: With *which* Christian church was the Romanian people born? According to the Orthodox, the

Greek Catholic Church was founded only in 1700, so it is the upstart. Moreover, some claim, until the Great Schism of 1054, there was only the Orthodox Church, the Catholic Church coming into existence in that year through its separation from Orthodoxy.[42] Greek Catholics contend that it was the *Orthodox* Church that came into being with the Schism, the original church being Roman Catholic, their own line; thus they see the formation of their church in 1700 as a *return* to the ancestral faith and not a departure.[43] Both sides can therefore claim that their believers hold to Romanians' "ancestral faith." This is an important point for anyone wishing to challenge the practice of religious conversion (see below).

Finally, each group accuses the other of having "non-Romanian" sympathies or connections. Greek Catholics present the Orthodox Church as having been much too cozy with the communists, including (in the early days) those "foreigners" Stalin and Zhdanov. The Orthodox hierarchy finds itself constantly on the defensive against this charge, made by its own faithful as well as by Greek Catholics. In addition, Greek Catholics view the Romanian Orthodox Church as too close to Russia—indeed, that church's fundamentalist current is firmly pro-Moscow, and Romanian Patriarch Teoctist has sided with Russian Patriarch Alexei on important matters. As for the international sympathies imputed to the Greek Catholic Church: while many of its admirers (including many Orthodox) see its ties with Rome as Romania's opening to the West, Orthodoxists[44] give this a more sinister spin: Greek Catholics are *agents* of the West, part of the anti-Romanian invasion of liberalism that will destroy true Romanian values. Worse still, Orthodox priestly propaganda advances the following false syllogism: Hungarians are Catholic, Greek Catholics are Catholic, therefore Greek Catholics are actually *Hungarians* (or at least Hungarian allies) working to separate Transylvania from Romania and rejoin it to Hungary.[45] Given that Transylvania's place in Hungary and Romania is a centuries-old sore point, Orthodox portrayal of Greek Catholics as "Hungarians" seriously diminishes Greek Catholic recruitment chances. Thus each side has its suspect "internationalism," from the other's point of view, and neither is afraid to use those connections to prevent the other from being seen as Chief Defender of the Romanian Nation.

Although both churches want a special relationship to Romanianness, the Orthodox Church has gone much further than the Greek Catholics in claiming it and in seeking to stigmatize the other faith as "non-Romanian." Writing of their church, Orthodox hierarchs pepper their prose with phrases like "the resentment of some against the Orthodox Church, which is of course the church of our nation" or "waves of enemies are rising up against the Romanian Orthodox Church and, through it, against the Romanian people."[46] In the March 1998 silent demonstration in Cluj at which Archbishop Anania prayed for the enemies of Romania and of the Orthodox Church (see above), the Romanian national flag and traditional identity symbols were prominent alongside the regalia of the church. The insistent identification of Orthodoxy with Romanianness accompanied portraying Greek Catholics as "other," "not-us."

How do these arguments connect to Inochentie's reburial? Because, according to people from both churches, each side wanted to claim him as primarily "ours" and not "the other's": they wanted to write him into their own versions of the national genealogy. For this, each side had to show itself the worthy heir of both Inochentie and the Romanian nation, enabling it to annex him at the other's expense. The dilemma was tricky on both sides. The Orthodox Church could claim him as theirs not in his speech or behavior but only in his possible *intentions* (his ostensible plan of returning to Orthodoxy). On the Greek Catholic side, there were two options, with different payoffs. If they presented him as chiefly a *Greek Catholic* hero, they would win fewer points for bringing him back (since few Romanians care about a Greek Catholic hero) than if they presented him as a *national* hero. But that claim opened Greek Catholics to the accusation of having divided the nation and weakened it.[47]

The politics around Inochentie thus show how alternative worlds of meaning were coming into conflict in the process of reordering them after the collapse of socialism. Two different churches had their respective versions of the nation's ancestry and their own place in it; both claimed Inochentie for their genealogy. Both sought to place different landmarks in the time line of the nation's biography (the Orthodox version would leave out the founding of Greek Catholicism altogether, if it could, while the Greek Catholics would make that event a centerpiece of Romanian history). They had in common an emphasis on the place of religious belief in Romanian national identity—this was what distinguished their versions of a national "world" from that of the Communist Party—as well as litmus tests for assessing the genuineness of that belief ("opportunism," "collaboration"). Over the long term, it is through these kinds of contests that the world of Romanian national identity will be gradually reordered.

Inochentie's Biography and the Question of Sentiment

Arguments over Inochentie concerned more than merely whose genealogy he would grace and whose history he would validate: his biography sparked various kinds of feelings and identifications as well. To bring in this subject takes our perception of his significance beyond the political maneuvering I have emphasized so far. In discussing Inochentie with Orthodox and Greek Catholic clergy and active Greek Catholic laypersons, I was surprised by the intense emotion they displayed: several of them became very angry, others of them wept.[48] I interpret these responses as evidence of a deep personal identification with the issues in the interchurch conflict. Talk of Inochentie's reburial served to focus the strong feelings involved. I believe certain aspects of his biography (his "résumé") favor this: his tireless work on behalf of the Romanian nation; the betrayal, exile, and personal suffering that resulted; and the unresolved question of Greek Catholicism's opportunistic founding.

As I have suggested elsewhere,[49] an inadequately understood aspect of national ideologies is how persons come to *feel* themselves "national"— how they cathect their nationness as part of their sense of self. To explore this subject would take me far afield from my purposes here, so I limit myself to the following brief points. First, in my research in Romania over three decades I have been struck by the importance of "exemplary biographies" of "remarkable men" in shaping Romanian national sentiment. (I believe this is true of other nationalisms as well.) Just as medieval Christians absorbed the exemplary lives of saints, so twentieth-century Romanians learn to identify with exemplary national heroes. Second, a crucial ingredient of Romanian (and other) national ideas is the notion of suffering and victimhood: Romanians as victimized and oppressed, usually by foreigners; Romanians as forever struggling for a recognition that is always denied them. Romania's exemplary heroes personify these ideas.

Courageous and brilliant, they frequently end in failure and suffering because their supporters betray them.[50] They tend to die unhappy deaths, often far from home, always struggling to affirm themselves and their nation in the eyes of the world. These exemplary lives condense the suffering, frustration, and sense of betrayal that are foundation stones of most Romanian history as taught in schools (excluding the proletarian bombast of the communist period), and they resonate with the suffering, frustration, and betrayal so many Romanians have experienced in recent times as well.[51]

For Romanians, Inochentie Micu is this kind of exemplary hero: he both personifies and symbolizes the Romanian nation, struggling for recognition and ultimately betrayed. All Romanians who have had these experiences and feel themselves patriotic can readily find themselves in Inochentie, and him in them. He thus further evokes the sentiment of national belonging that he was so instrumental in shaping, and he does so in a very personal way. An Orthodox priest explained this connection to me in expressing his satisfaction at Inochentie's impending return: "He was a martyr of Romanians. This isn't just a religious issue: we *should* be bringing these values home—Titulescu came back to Braşov, but [we should] also [bring composer] George Enescu, [historian of religion] Mircea Eliade, [philosopher] Emil Cioran, [playwright] Eugen Ionesco. It's natural to want to recuperate our national symbols, and that's what those people are: they made 'being Romanian' a matter of personal identification." All Romanians, then, Orthodox as well as Greek Catholic, can identify with Inochentie the national martyr.

He is a particularly potent symbol, however, for Greek Catholics, victimized by the Communist Party despite their religion's crucial role in achieving Romanian independence. His life evokes their years of underground existence and sacrifice, the imprisonments and even deaths of their loved ones. In his reburial service, speakers drew a direct parallel between his life of suffering and exile and that of Greek Catholic Bishop Iuliu Hossu, who died in a communist jail after twenty-two years of imprisonment; this facilitated similar comparisons for others present. Inochentie's steadfastness in defense of the faith, evident from his correspondence in exile, impels them toward firmly defending that faith now. (At the same time, the question of "opportunism" and national betrayal gnaws at the innards of those Greek Catholics who turned Orthodox or Roman Catholic after 1948, despite the courageous example of their bishops. For them, his return is an occasion for self-doubt—but even that means connecting one's own life with his.) It is no wonder that talk of Inochentie arouses deep feeling for those active in his return. He is a richly ambiguous, powerful, and complex symbol having multiple emotional resonances.

In short, Inochentie's biography exemplifies and condenses Greek Catholics' own persecution and suffering; it encourages an intense emotional relationship with him. To bring him home is a kind of compensation, a restitution of their own personal pasts and their sense of the worthiness of their church. As one lay activist said to me, taking part in his homecoming was a peak experience in her life. Standing in the Blaj cathedral, she felt all around her a joyous, triumphant feeling: "He was exiled, but in the end he won! And so will we!" Inochentie awakens the sentiments of Orthodox Romanians for his patriotic struggle, but for Greek Catholics he arouses far more: an intimate reliving and validation of their having suffered not for their national identity but for their religious convictions. For the two worlds of these faiths, he reorders identity in dissimilar ways.

Competition in the Religious Market

Still other reorderings intersected in Inochentie's reburial, as many people responded to postsocialist upheaval by seeking comfort in religious renewal. What religion might they find most helpful? Their search leads us to consider yet another form of competition between Romania's Orthodox and Greek Catholic churches, besides their vying for church properties and a privileged relationship to Romanian national identity. This larger competition subsumes the other two: it is the competition for souls. I use this language, and speak of a religious "market," for two reasons: first, because Romanians active in religious life themselves use this language to account for what they see around them, and second, because I find in it a very apt analogy for processes that the collapse of communist parties unleashed in religious life.

With the end of official atheism in Eastern Europe and the former Soviet Union came not only much confusion but also a new freedom of worship. These caused something like market competition among different faiths both within and external to each country. Some churches and clergy saw the religious opening as a chance to win new converts; their attitude resembled that of Western firms seeing the former Soviet bloc as awash with potential customers for their goods. From the Orthodox point of view, however, the religious market was already saturated—by Orthodoxy. Other religions began testing to see if this was in fact true. The Orthodox-Greek Catholic conflicts over property and national identity directly concerned this competition for souls: in claiming to be the true national church and in fighting over buildings, each church was positioning itself to expand and care properly for its congregation.[52] The field containing their competition is, however, much wider: besides the Orthodox and Greek Catholic churches on which I concentrate here, it includes Roman Catholics and various forms of fundamentalist Protestants, especially Seventh Day Adventists, Baptists, Pentecostals, Mormons, Jehovah's Witnesses, and so on.[53] Most of these are based abroad.

As I read various publications and listened to people talk, I was struck by the prevalence of competition as a theme—often discussed using the term *proselytism*. Competing for souls is a matter of how churches build followings, a matter with many possible solutions. Consider, for instance, views on what "faith" is and how one acquires it. Is one irrevocably born into a faith (that is, does one inherit one's faith?), or can one acquire it through persuasion and conversion? If people convert, is it from genuine conviction or, rather, from opportunism and situational tactics? As I explained above, the Orthodox Church and the Greek Catholic Church can each present itself as Romanians' "ancestral faith," and the other as deviant or derivative. In my experience, however, the idea that faith is inherited is more likely to appear among Orthodox than Greek Catholics[54] (who did in fact change their religious affiliation in the early 1700s, even if some now justify it as a return to the ancestral faith).

Accompanying this difference between faith as inherited versus as chosen are other differences. To emphasize conversion and choice means to privilege *interior* states (belief, conviction) of *individuals*; the Orthodox Church, by contrast, emphasizes faith as a matter of *customary group practice*. Emphasis on conversion and inner belief makes faith a matter of choice among religions on offer in an economy of faiths and religious interests—in other words, in a religious market. Here is where Orthodoxy perceives proselytism as a threat: if faith is *not* customary group practice but individual conviction, then Orthodox souls can be seduced away by evangelization. In this kind of competitive "market," the Orthodox Church is at a decided disadvantage: having maintained its position for centuries as the ally of the state, it lacks a missionizing tradition. In consequence, its clerics tend to see any kind of competition as "unfair," as in this revealing comment made to me by an Orthodox monk:

> In [current] circumstances, our believers can easily be stolen, especially because of the techniques the neo-Protestants use—careful listening, attention to people's feelings, a very personal approach [KV: And a suitable social message]. Yes. Neo-Protestants shouldn't be coming here in a moment of crisis! It's unfair competition!

It is in the context of competition that one might interpret the frequently aired question of "opportunism," which serves as a means of devaluing the moral claims (and therefore the recruitment ability) of the other church. An Orthodox-inspired standard historiography has long presented the eighteenth-century founding of the Greek Catholic Church as opportunistic, its adherents converting for privileges rather than from belief; this argument still appears, such as in a 1998 article by an Orthodox bishop that asked just how Catholic Inochentie's successors were.[55] Indeed, it is only this argument that enables the Orthodox Church to reclaim Inochentie Micu through his putative intention of returning to Orthodoxy when the privileges failed to materialize. If Greek Catholicism was born of opportunism, then the Orthodox Church holds the moral upper hand in its quest to retain its religious monopoly. More broadly, if that church can classify *any* departure from the ancestral faith as opportunistic, then it has a safeguard against the defection of its faithful in the new religious market.

Greek Catholics find the charge of opportunism deeply disturbing. As one elderly priest said, telling me of his twelve years in communist jails, "If Inochentie became a Greek Catholic only for material benefits and had no faith [i.e., if he did not believe the fundamental Greek Catholic dogma of the primacy of the pope as the sole heir of Peter, the "rock" upon whom Christ founded his church], then all our suffering in prison was for naught. Inochentie the opportunist wipes out Greek Catholicism's entire raison d'être." For this man, the best counterargument is the unbending resistance of the Greek Catholic bishops and other clergy to communist blandishments after 1948, proving their genuine conviction and highly *in*opportune integrity. Having such proof, in turn, enables Greek Catholics to make their own charges of opportunism against the Orthodox Church, which survived the communist period by open compromise with the Communist Party. They are quick to point out that Inochentie Micu, by contrast, preferred exile and the loss of his position as bishop rather than betray either his nation or his faith. By holding up a strong moral example, Greek Catholics hope to attract people disaffected with Orthodoxy.

In considering these kinds of arguments, I discerned two general attitudes toward competition. One of them promoted greater openness in the market for souls and encouraged proselytizing (an attitude more characteristic of Greek and Roman Catholics and fundamentalist Protestants). The other resisted "market penetration" and competition, condemned proselytism, and strove to maintain a communist-style monopoly of the religious market by political means (this tended to be the Orthodox approach). The latter attitude particularly affects the relation of religion to secular authority (hence, how authority may be sacralized), for monopolizing the religious market may entail achieving a privileged relation with state power.

One means of retarding religious market forces is, as already discussed, to promote faith as a matter of inheritance rather than choice; another is political action to prevent the growth of other churches, as I showed in discussing the property question. In addition, some in the Orthodox Church strive to make it de facto or de jure the state religion.[56] Here are some examples. First, in the summer of 1996, the Jehovah's Witnesses held their world congress in Bucharest. This sect (unlike others, such as Baptists and Seventh Day Adventists) had been banned entirely in the communist period for its refusal to respect nation-state loyalties. Yet after 1989 it began acquiring followers in Romania at a considerable rate (sometimes buying them outright with goods and money). The Witnesses' congress drew much controversy in the Romanian press, including complaints that housing the participants would displace students who were Orthodox faithful. Matters worsened when two people were killed in a scuffle outside the meeting hall. At this point, Patriarch Teoctist (probably seizing on negative public sentiment against a group he saw as a major problem) demanded that Romania's Parliament pass a law making the Orthodox Church the official national church. His demand was not satisfied,[57] but the point was established: a church-state monopoly would save Romanians from unwanted proselytism and the Orthodox Church from unwelcome competition.

A similar view appears in a 1997 article entitled "Proselytism and Democracy," signed by Orthodox Archbishop Daniel of Iaşi. The article begins thus: "The intensification of religious proselytizing in Romania on the part of certain sects and associations supported financially and morally by religious organizations in the West is creating increased discontent in the population." This observation leads him to query the relationship between proselytizing and democracy:

> While some practitioners and supporters of religious proselytizing, especially Americans, justify it as part of religious freedom and democracy, for Romanians and many other Europeans proselytism and the religious conflicts it produces constitute not a sign of democracy but a threat to it.

He then calls for a law on religion that would limit religious activity to those faiths that treat other faiths respectfully, excluding "provocational and aggressive proselytizing that uses any means—financial, economic, psychological and political pressure—in order to convert or to buy souls in a kind of religious-ideological colonialism over souls that cannot sufficiently defend themselves."[58] Archbishop Daniel, possible future patriarch, thus seeks new laws to prevent aggressive competition, which weakened Orthodox souls might be unprepared to resist.

In their most extreme form, these monopolist designs rest on fully identifying the Romanian Orthodox Church not just with the state but with the Romanian *nation*, and other faiths with "foreign invasion." For example, an Orthodox monk exhorts Romanians not to leave the true faith; he lists several of the greatest figures in Romanian history and declares dramatically that they were not Baptists, Adventists, or Jehovah's Witnesses, "these crazy religions that have appeared nowadays. Not a sect existed in our country back then. These people come from abroad, paid by Freemasons, to spoil our true faith and our origins and roots as an Orthodox people." He continues:

> Don't run off after the slaves of satan, who come from the West with millions of dollars. They buy those who are stupid and uninformed about religion, to divide the unity and the soul of the Romanian nation. . . . Stay away from these crazy people! . . . We must keep to the beliefs held by all our great princes and forefathers and all true Romanians. If you want to be a true son of Christ and of Romania, hold to the righteous faith, Orthodoxy, which we have had for 2,000 years. If not, you are no son of Christ or of the Church, and you are alien to the Romanian nation. You cannot be a Christian Romanian citizen if you don't have the righteous faith in Christ. You're foreign. You are not a son of our country . . . . We were born Orthodox from the beginning, we have been Orthodox for 2,000 years, and we must stay Orthodox until death.[59]

In this way the author asserts an essential, organic connection between Orthodoxy and not just the state but the very survival of Romanians as a people; this makes proselytism tantamount to denationalization, and conversion a form of treason.

Reorganizing World Religions

The above examples indicate, I believe, some of the means by which a large state-socialist monopoly, the Romanian Orthodox Church, has reacted to the entry of competitor faiths into a regionwide market for active religious worship. Moreover, the examples illuminate events in Russia, which show that I am not overstating the case when I see the Orthodox Church as striving to perpetuate its monopoly and reduce competition. The Russian events connect to Inochentie because of what Greek Catholicism means to suspicious Russian clergy.

In September 1997, Russia's Duma passed a law on religions. This law granted different faiths greater or lesser privileges according to their previous status in the Soviet Union. Special rights went to any religion that had been formally recognized fifteen years before: these included Orthodoxy, Judaism, Islam, and Buddhism. Excluded were Roman Catholicism, evangelical Christian denominations, and dissident Orthodox sects. Religions in the first, privileged group can own property, have radio and TV stations, be tax-exempt, run schools, distribute religious literature, and invite foreigners to come and preach. None of the lower-tier faiths has these rights; they cannot proselytize or do any of the things essential to building a stable congregation.[60] Although President Yeltsin initially criticized this proposal, he ultimately signed it—having caved in, according to his critics, to pressure from the Russian Orthodox hierarchy, which viewed other groups as threatening its influence.[61] The *New York Times* noted that the Vatican had protested the measure on several occasions; the report discussed the upsurge in religious activity within Russia that was causing the Orthodox Church to solidify its position as the dominant religion, the new law serving to protect it from foreign competitors.[62]

The events I have described suggest that the end of Communist Party rule generated the following global process. Into a world Christendom in which ecumenism had been a buzzword for several decades came the Russian Orthodox Church, newly released from its communist shackles. Its eighty million adherents, most of them lacking adequate religious instruction, were fair game for other Christian groups formerly excluded from proselytizing there.[63] The church hierarchy, however, firmly intended to keep them under its control. The result was a four-way contest, as the Russian Orthodox Church tried to forestall incursions into Russian territory by Roman Catholics and various Protestants, and to contest the dominance of world Orthodoxy with the Orthodox Church in Constantinople (especially its patriarch, Bartholomew, considered Orthodoxy's primus inter pares). We might well describe the situation with the following image: three major centers of hierarchical religious organization—Moscow, Constantinople, and Rome—and their three leaders—Patriarch Alexei II, Patriarch Bartholomew, and Pope John Paul II—are locked in a struggle much like that of the Russian, Ottoman, and Habsburg dynasts across the same space three centuries ago, while (now, as then) a variety of Protestants flood the postsocialist religious market using less centralized, more egalitarian tactics.

In the three-way struggle of the hierarchs, the Catholic Church has the advantage of a relatively monolithic organization and a single head for its billion members, whereas Orthodoxy is divided among fifteen rivalrous independent centers. The rejuvenation of Russian Orthodoxy animates these rivalries, enabling the Russian patriarch to challenge Constantinople's Patriarch Bartholomew for leadership of the world's 250 million Orthodox. Resuscitating Moscow's past role as the "Third Rome" (the center of Christendom after the fall first of Rome itself and then of Constantinople), Patriarch Alexei has set himself up as an alternative center of gravity for other Orthodox patriarchs, such as the Romanian, Bulgarian, Serbian, Slovak, and Ukrainian. A number of them believe that Constantinople Patriarch Bartholomew is too receptive to the West.[64] Perhaps Alexei's defiance explains why, after years of Constantinople's ecumenical rapprochement with Catholicism, Patriarch Bartholomew gave several signs during 1997 of putting distance between himself and the pope, thereby dampening John Paul's hopes for a Catholic-Orthodox reconciliation by the year 2000.[65]

If Alexei is challenging Bartholomew for leadership of the Eastern Orthodox population, his struggle with the Roman Catholic Church is even more intense, and it is here that Greek Catholicism suddenly looms large despite its small numbers. Since Vatican II, the Vatican's official policy has been that Roman Catholicism and Orthodoxy are "sister" churches, and that Catholic attempts to proselytize among the Orthodox are out of bounds. This policy distinguishes today's Catholic Church from that of, say, Habsburg days; it has been revised and reiterated several times with specific reference to the situation in post-1989 Eastern Europe and Russia. Official policy notwithstanding, however, some Roman Catholic clergy continue to missionize among Russia's Orthodox population.[66] The Russian Orthodox hierarchy suspects even more such activity, viewing the Greek Catholic revival in Ukraine and adjacent regions as Rome's way of insinuating Roman Catholicism into Russia. Exacerbating the problem is the question of church properties.[67]

Further evidence of these competitive struggles among the three churches comes from events surrounding the second European Ecumenical Assembly, held in Graz, Austria, June 23-29, 1997. Organized as a gathering for dialogue (not decision-making), the Assembly was titled "Reconciliation, Gift of God and Beginning of a New Life." Among the issues to be discussed was the vexed question of Greek Catholic church buildings in Orthodox countries. Around the time of this gathering it was hoped that the first-ever meeting between Pope John Paul II and Patriarch

Alexei II might take place, toward further reconciliation of the two churches. Nine days before the meeting, however, Alexei canceled it on the grounds that preparations were insufficient.[68] Those Orthodox leaders who did attend the assembly took a hard-line approach to the Catholic Church, thereby scuttling the hoped-for reconciliation. When I discussed these events with an Orthodox monk in Bucharest, he responded: "Patriarch Alexei's actions are very important. The pope has to know there's another powerful man who's head of a church; the pope can't just push him around, draw him into his own plans." "Is this why Alexei refused to meet him?" I asked. "Yes! There's just too much Roman Catholic proselytizing!" In any event, after the Assembly the Vatican reaffirmed its policy of "nonaggression,"[69] stating that it will not pursue reconciliation through Uniatism (mixing Catholic doctrine with Orthodox ritual) and that Roman Catholic priests will go to Russia solely to minister to Catholic populations there, not to proselytize the Orthodox.[70]

The competition between Catholic and Eastern Orthodox churches is felt on Transylvanian soil as well. First, new Greek and Roman Catholic church buildings are springing up all over, many assisted by funds from "sister" Roman Catholic parishes in Germany, Italy, Switzerland, and France.[71] Second, perhaps following the lead of Patriarch Alexei, Romania's Patriarch Teoctist declined to schedule a visit with the pope despite an official invitation by the Romanian government.[72] Third has been reorganizations of the Catholic administrative hierarchy. In 1991 the pope raised the Transylvanian city Alba Iulia from the rank of diocese to archdiocese, subject directly to the Vatican rather than to Bucharest. Eventually Transylvania's other Catholic dioceses may be subordinated to Alba Iulia and not to Bucharest, thus redistributing Catholic power away from the Romanian Orthodox capital and concentrating it in Transylvania (home of most of Romania's Catholics).[73] Despite protests against that change, the pope then made the Greek Catholic bishop of Alba Iulia a cardinal in 1992. Once again, as in the eighteenth century, imperial strivings under the guise of world religions intersect in Transylvania.

We've heard nothing from Inochentie Micu for quite some time, but in fact he has been here all along. It is partly the global shift in the balance of religious forces, I believe, that has finally brought to fruition the idea of bringing him home, whereas it failed earlier in the twentieth century. These international forces unleashed a tremendous contest between Greek Catholicism's two "parents," world Catholicism and world Orthodoxy. In those circumstances, Romania's Greek Catholics were suddenly able to gain control of the bones of a great national hero who happened to be theirs. Perhaps the desperateness of their situation—years of interdiction, aging adherents, Orthodox obstruction of their property ownership— gave them unprecedented energy. And perhaps facilitating Inochentie's move was the presence of Greek Catholics in Romania's government at the precise moment when worldwide Catholic-Orthodox relations were com- ing to a head. Thus, by bringing Inochentie home, Greek Catholics could show themselves a force to be reckoned with. Without the resurgence of Russian Orthodoxy, however, widely encouraging anti-Western, anti- Catholic attitudes and resistance on the property question, Pope John Paul II might not have been moved to concur in Inochentie's repatriation. His travels were perhaps overdetermined, but the pope had the final word.

INOCHENTIE COMES HOME

How was Inochentie to navigate his way through the storm of religious controversy and land safely at his final resting place in Blaj? With two churches eagerly claiming him as ancestor and many possible agendas rid- ing on the outcome (reconciliation? a triumph for Greek Catholics at the expense of Orthodox?), the plans for his return proved controversial. One proposal would have moved his bones from Rome to Romania's capital, Bucharest, for display; after viewing by the Romanian public and a solemn Mass, he would be taken first on a tour through villages in Transylvania that had played an important part in Greek Catholic history, then to the town of Blaj for reburial in the cathedral he had founded. In both Bucharest and Blaj he would be treated with much pomp and ceremony. This might be called the "conciliatory variant," inasmuch as it would have given both Orthodox and Greek Catholic spiritual capitals some time with him. According to one Greek Catholic advocate of this view, the whole point of bringing Inochentie home was to expose *all* Romanians to the true history of that church and what it stood for, to counteract forty years of misleading Orthodox and communist propaganda.[74]

Another proposal, however, had him going straight from Rome to Blaj, for a simple burial. The argument was that because Inochentie had had absolutely nothing to do with either Bucharest or its Orthodox patriarchate, he had no reason to put in an appearance there. The Greek Catholic priest who told me of this plan claimed that it had been selected because "too many people [i.e., too many Orthodox] are trying to get in on the act, and besides, it's inappropriate to put victims together with their torturers in a single pot." I call this proposal for Inochentie's return the "intransigent Greek Catholic" variant.

At the time of my research the plans were still uncertain; in late October 1997, however, I learned that the reburial had just taken place.[75] Inochentie had gone in a special limousine straight from Rome to Blaj, avoiding Bucharest; the intransigent Greek Catholic variant had prevailed. He was received in Blaj with a solemn Mass during which, some participants believed, they felt the palpable presence of his spirit rejoicing to be home at last.[76]

As for the reburial itself, that event, too, was very much a Greek Catholic one. At the three-day scholarly symposium preceding it, Inochentie's Greek Catholic identity was much stressed, and there were even hints at a deep enmity between him and the Orthodox Church.[77] About ten thousand people, largely Greek Catholics, attended the reburial. Many of them were schoolchildren bused in from all across Transylvania. Celebrants at the reburial included nearly all high-level Greek Catholic clerics from Romania and other countries, dignitaries from the Vatican, but no Romanian Orthodox clergy; the patriarchate's episcopal vicar from Bucharest was present only as a delegate of Teoctist and the Holy Synod, not as a celebrant.[78] Others in attendance were a delegate from the Romanian president, parliamentarians from the National Peasant Party, and county authorities.[79] Speeches at the event, as well as subsequent reports (following the points emphasized by the speakers), underscored both Inochentie's unshaken faith and his role as a great national hero who opened the way to Romanian liberation. A procession of Greek Catholic priests circled the town square, carrying his coffin draped with the Romanian flag.

Perhaps from Orthodox pressure, however, wider coverage of the event was sparse—a brief clip on the evening news, summary mention in the press.[80] By monopolizing Inochentie, the Greek Catholics had narrowed his embrace. To rebury an ancestor is to create a community of mourners. That community might be more restrictive (mostly Greek Catholics) or more inclusive (Greek Catholics together with Orthodox, as sons of Inochentie's Romanian nation). In reburying him as *their particular* ancestor, Greek Catholics limited the meaningful community of living and dead to their own congregation. We might say that they localized him excessively.[81] Moreover, they resignified space in a very local way as well, sanctifying with his bones only a small, Greek Catholic space—his cathedral in Blaj—rather than a larger territory of Romanianness, such as the Greater Serbia claimed by the more ambulatory bones of Serbia's Prince Lazar in 1987–1989.

Nonetheless, it was precisely because he overflows these narrow confines that Inochentie was able to return at all: were he not also a prominent national hero, the Orthodox Church would surely have blocked his repatriation. Despite Greek Catholicism's monopoly, he came home as both religious and national ancestor. His homecoming partakes of the global trend I mentioned in chapter 1: the return of heritage or cultural treasure. Inochentie Micu is one such cultural treasure: no matter what side you take, he had a tremendous impact on the emancipation of Romanians from foreign rule. Thus, he is a notable icon in the broad "sacred space" of Romanian national identity.[82] Moreover, he is a particularly consequential cultural treasure for postsocialist times, because his homecoming publicly reshapes Romanian identity as bound up with *religious faith*, an aspect of Romanianness that was necessarily suppressed in the communist period.[83] He therefore makes a signal contribution to reordering the "world" of Romania's self-image as no longer an ostensibly godless land.

Thinking of Inochentie as cultural treasure suggests a reason why he had to wait so long to come home. It is only our present era of "globalization," with its concomitant localizing and place-making practices, that brings back to their places of origin so many cultural treasures like him. In other words, globalization doesn't just *accompany* localizing practices: it makes them possible. I wish to dwell briefly on Inochentie's place-making qualities, so as to complete the arc I inaugurated with his highly localized sarcophagus in Rome.

The moment Inochentie set out from Rome, he began a journey of particularization. In Rome he was part of a cosmopolitan community dedicated to serving a universalist, international Catholic Church. Within that community he was known for his work on behalf of the universal faith; his Romanian origin was inconsequential there. His move to Transylvania particularized him, making his Catholicism *Greek* and his identity *Romanian.* He could become a meaningful ancestor for those who brought him home only by redefining his point of reference as local. The very notion of "homecoming" reveals his particularistic side, as we see from the distinctly localizing language that presented his bones as properly resting *at home*. Several people with whom I discussed him used this kind of language—"The guy's gotta come home" (*omu' trebuie să vină acasă*)—as did newspaper reports of his reburial.[84] For Romanians, Inochentie represents a major and very Romanian value. He should be revered on his native soil; and only there, it seems, can he be revered fittingly.

Here, perhaps, ideas about repatriated cultural treasure may come together with cosmic ideas about death, proper burial, and resurrection. It is not just a matter of burying "our sons" on "our soil." Inochentie himself saw the connection as deeper, believing that at the Last Judgment, "only from the soil of your homeland [*patria*] can you rise from the dead."[85] His reburial in Blaj thus fuses the patriotic with the sacred motives for repatriating him as treasure, sanctifying a particular space (Blaj) for times past, present, and future, as both Greek Catholic and Romanian. And might it be that because Inochentie is simultaneously ancestor, saint, and national hero, his reburial (like those involving other properly tended ancestors) will evoke his protection of the people who honor him? Perhaps the belated honoring of his remains will enable him to protect the nation to whose improvement he dedicated his life, and even to accomplish a gradual reconciliation of the quarrels dividing it.

CONCLUSION

What have I accomplished in this chapter, besides introducing an unusual Transylvanian with acute national consciousness and steadfast faith, as well as great political talent? First, tracking Inochentie's bones has revealed an unexpected feature of postsocialist transformation. I have shown that it is not only Coke and Pepsi that see the postsocialist bloc as an open field for market competition: something similar is going on among world religions, especially among the Roman Catholic and Protestant churches with respect to the Eastern Orthodox realm. The response of the Orthodox churches (i.e., to shore up their monopoly by attempting to create a special relationship with state authorities) aligns them with nationalist forces in each Orthodox country that oppose Western market penetration of all kinds.

Second, I have shown how these bones entered into Romania's new political arena. A possible means for interchurch reconciliation and national strengthening, they were drawn into postsocialist conflicts over property, national identity, and religious renewal. In part, Inochentie owes this fate to his multivocality: much of his recent life as a symbol comes from his complex eighteenth-century résumé, which made him open to different readings from the Orthodox and Greek Catholic points of view. Both readings make him an ancestor, but of different kinds. For Greek Catholics he is a founder of their religion, a mobilizer of their nationality, a link with their Roman cousins and with Western Catholicism more generally, and a forebear who sacrificed his title for his principles. For the Orthodox, he is but one of a longer line of clever ancestors who could dissemble their beliefs in order to defend and promote the national and religious cause. Though he used Greek Catholicism to secure privileges for Romanians, he surely remained true to his own forefathers in covertly retaining the ancestral faith.

Inochentie's reburial has proved to be an excellent vantage point for examining how worlds are being reordered in postsocialist Romania. Through him we have seen efforts to redefine church-state relations and property ownership, ideas of morality and just compensation, social relations and national identities. We have seen him resignify Romania's space—first, by endowing a small Transylvanian town with even more sacrality than it had before, and second by *not* treading a lengthier path to Bucharest. The reburial also resignified time by revising Romanian history: it augmented the role of Catholicism in that history far more than had been allowed under socialism, and accordingly diminished the role of Orthodoxy; it restored to public currency the suppressed names of Greek Catholics martyred for their beliefs; and, perhaps most important, it returned to Romanian history the idea that Romanians are a people whose historical identity is thoroughly permeated with religious faith.

All these themes contribute to my project of animating the study of postsocialist politics by seeking to grasp its many-layered meanings. In this chapter I have emphasized the details of politicking around Inochentie Micu; in the next, I give more attention to the themes of ancestors, proper burial, and time and space. Both chapters reveal the significance of dead bodies by treating them as points at which processes of global scope intersect with lower-level ones. In this way, I show that macro and micro exist not as separate instances but in their encounter in the events that give dead bodies political life. By assuming that the macro is *in* the micro (and vice versa), I have found that a modest set of bones can open up the world.

Serbia is wherever there are Serbian graves.
—VUK DRAŠKOVIĆ

CHAPTER THREE

Giving Proper Burial, Reconfiguring Space and Time

I began this book with a number of politically significant bones and corpses, along with some general ideas about how one might think about them. In chapter 2, by contrast, I discussed at length a single set of bones, summarizing the powerful forces that moved Inochentie Micu from his first to his second grave site. I focused on political conflicts around property, national identity, and global religious competition, asking how various religious groups sought to incorporate him into Romanian national genealogies. Although I spoke of ideas about proper burial and reconfiguring space and time (additional themes from chapter 1), they took second place to those other topics.

In the present chapter I alter my strategy once again. I look at some examples from what used to be Yugoslavia, placing more emphasis than before on the politics of national conflict, the creation of new states, and

the concomitant reconfiguring of space and time (that is, on altering the
significance of territory and on rewriting history). Whereas in chapter 2
I used concepts to analyze a case, in this one I use disparate case material to illustrate concepts, gradually moving away from the cases toward
a more abstract discussion of dead-body politics and reconfiguring time.
My dead bodies here are, unlike Inochentie Micu, largely nameless; their
work in cosmic reordering is mediated by ideas about kinship and ancestor worship, mortuary practices, and space and time. Finally, the two
chapters differ in their form: in contrast with chapter 2, which was organized loosely around a chronology (Inochentie's pre- and postmortem
lives) combined with a spatial move from local upward to global and
back again, this chapter works more like a loom, interweaving its themes
by repetition and shifts of emphasis, and by ranging back and forth
among horizontally equivalent sites. I hope the effect of this difference
will contribute to my message about contrasting organizations of space
and time.

I choose post-Yugoslavia because there is no better instance for seeing
the complexity of the interlinked themes I want to explore. That complexity, however, makes the case difficult both to describe and to generalize
from. Therefore, I will spell out more fully than I did for Inochentie Micu
what makes post-Yugoslav dead-body politics unique (underscoring my
point that there is no single rule for how to analyze these phenomena).[1] I
use the term "Yugoslavia" to refer only to the entity that existed before the
secession of Slovenia and Croatia in 1991, not to the Serbian state that subsequently usurped that name; to speak collectively about the new states
there, I use "post-Yugoslav." A brief reminder: Yugoslavia was a federation consisting of republics—Croatia, Serbia, Slovenia, Macedonia, and so
forth—some of which became separate states and all of which had different ethnonational groups intermingled on their territories.

The obvious difference between Yugoslavia and most other cases in the
region is that not only did a hegemonic Party collapse, but so did the entire
state, through warfare aimed at creating several new successor states.[2] That
process involved, first, territorial revisions aimed at reducing each republic's multiethnicity and, second, even more thoroughgoing revisions of
history than occurred in other places. The revisions not only decommu-
nized history (the main tendency elsewhere) but also created specifically

national histories suited to consolidating new nation-states. In speaking of post-Yugoslav nation-state creation, I should emphasize, I do not see it (unlike much popular writing) as "resuscitating" old enmities that communism had "suppressed." Rather, post-1989 nationalism was the product of Yugoslavia's own organization, which *reinforced* national identities by making them the basis for the federal republics.[3] Already in the 1970s problems were arising from this solution, and they worsened after Tito's death in 1980.

Another thing specific to the post-Yugoslav cases is what we might call a very intense burial regime. First, even before the breakup, one had to pay rent on grave sites of kin buried in cemeteries; the fee went to the Yugoslav state, and if it wasn't paid, the burial site would be leased to someone else (doubtless with the contents removed). Pamela Ballinger has described the disruptive effects of this practice for Italians exiled from Istria by the formation of communist Yugoslavia in 1945.[4] The practice has been retained, with the successor states now getting the fees. Second, people hold strong ideas about proper burial and about continuing relations with dead kin; frequent visits to tombs are common; and violence against enemy graves has a history at least as old as World War II. I will expand upon this point below.

Also specific to the post-Yugoslav cases is a distinctive patterning in how dead bodies enter politics: the *nameless* dead have been of equal if not greater importance, compared with the famous heroes common to my other examples. In consequence, I will devote most of this chapter to them, leaving the famous aside. Post-Yugoslavs, too, have reburied some famous dead,[5] such as Prince Lazar (mentioned in the introduction), but in addition they have reburied with much ceremony thousands of plain citizens found scattered in various unmarked burial sites—persons whose names are known only to their families, friends, and neighbors. There are two kinds of post-Yugoslav nameless dead: those from World War II and those from the present fighting. Rediscoveries of World War II dead helped to ignite warfare in 1991, which yielded still other bodies in mass graves, sources of recrimination that fueled the wars further.[6]

These specificities of the post-Yugoslav cases—new nation-state formation, strong feelings about relations between dead and living, and the role of nameless dead—give a unique coloring to the place of these dead bodies in reordering meaningful worlds, and particularly to their reconfiguring space and time. Concerning space, burial and reburial are a matter of *earth*, of digging into the very dust of the spaces and territories in which the bodies lie. To establish new successor nation-states means to mark territories as "ours" by discovering "our sons" in mass graves and giving them proper burial in "our soil," thus consecrating the respective space as "ours." Owing to the interspersal of ethnic groups within post-Yugoslavia, however, what are now "our" territories with "our" dead also contain dead who are "alien." Thus fixing and consecrating the boundaries of "our" soil has been a nasty, bloody process. That process is part of what I call reshaping or reconfiguring space. Vuk Drašković, Serbian nationalist and leader of the opposition to dictator Slobodan Milošević, put it succinctly. "Serbia is wherever there are Serbian graves."[7]

Post-Yugoslav corpses have also aided in reshaping time. The six-hundred-year-old bones of Prince Lazar, borne from monastery to monastery throughout all the areas containing Serbs, not only established the territorial claims of a new Serbian state. They also compressed time, as if his death in 1389 had occurred just a few days ago. In this way the new Serbia was rejoined with its days of glory as the first medieval state formed in Southeastern Europe, prior to the Ottoman conquest. Reburying Vlatko Maček in Zagreb reconnected the new Croatia with precommunist (1930s) politics, as if the communist period had not existed. The same excising takes place by reburying the dead of World War II precisely as new dead are being produced in their name. To prepare the way for a lengthier treatment of how Yugoslav bodies reconfigure space and time, I will briefly show their role in how the wars began.

FORMER YUGOSLAVIA, LAND OF GRAVES

If, in chapter two, Transylvania was the epicenter of tectonic shifts in relations among Catholics, Orthodox, and Protestants, the space that was Yugoslavia occupies the same position for *multiple* intersections: of Eastern and Western Christianity with Islam, of "East" and "West" more broadly, of "communism" and "capitalism," communism and fascism. It is also the land of political corpses without number, lying in limestone

caves, mass graves, and other sites all across the landscape. As shown in
the work of anthropologists Pamela Ballinger, Bette Denich, and Robert
Hayden, the skeletal inhabitants of limestone caves were the first troops
mobilized in the Yugoslav wars.[8] They were mobilized for a campaign to
revise recent history.

Briefly, the subject being revised was multiple massacres committed by
numerous groups during the latter part of World War II. The most important perpetrators were Croatian fascists—known as the Ustaša—against
Serbs and the communist underground ("partisans"); partisans against
fascists and others in their way; and Serbian royalists (Četniks) against
partisans, Muslims, and some Croats.[9] Mass slaughter occurred on all
sides, the victims being thrown into caves or buried in shallow mass graves
or simply left to rot. Here is a short description concerning one specific
episode, from Yugoslav Communist Party leader Milovan Djilas in his
memoir *Wartime*:

> The number exceed[ed] twenty thousand. . . . A year or two later
> there was grumbling in the Slovene Central Committee that they
> had trouble with the peasants from those areas, because under-
> ground rivers were casting up bodies. They also said that piles of
> corpses were heaving up as they rotted in shallow mass graves, so
> that the very earth seemed to breathe.[10]

At the war's end and with the installation of Tito's regime, all specific
mention of these massacres was suppressed; they could be spoken of only
in the abstract categories "victims of fascism" and "domestic traitors."[11]
Monuments were raised to the abstract "victims of fascism," but no one
was to name or to see to the proper burial of their own particular dead.
Most especially, there was no mention at all (except quietly, within families) of the murders carried out by communist partisans. The silencing of
this grim subject meant that none of the murders could be avenged (very
important, in this area), and so neither the souls of these dead nor the
minds of those close to them could rest in peace.

As the regime began to weaken in the late 1980s, however, bit by bit
those people who knew where their dead lay began opening graves and
giving the victims proper burials. Significantly, and unlike most reburi-

als of the famous, these involved numerous people in local communities, drawn directly into the process of handling the dead. In addition, they involved even larger numbers indirectly, as some of the exhumations and reburials were filmed and shown on television. Films widely viewed in Serbia, for instance, showed people digging out bones from the caves, placing the bones in plastic bags, and handing the bags up into the light. The bags were then passed down long lines of villagers, each of whom held them (see plate 19), making direct contact with long-dead relatives and friends; the camera recorded their deep emotions for a national audience.

Bette Denich shows how nationalist politicians, taking stock of these events, used them to feed a growing nationalist frenzy.[17] Attention centered on the question of culpability, as different groups claimed various dead as "ours," massacred by "communists" or "Serbs" or "Ustaša." Seeking political support, nationalist politicians raised questions as to how many had been massacred on each side and who was most at fault. Finding the skeletons of those whom communist partisans had killed, for instance, was instrumental in building the anticommunist sentiment that assured the

19 Exhumation of skeletons of Serbian dead from limestone caves in Croatia, 1991 (shown on Serbian television). The bag in the foreground contains bones.

victory of Franjo Tudjman's nationalist party in the first Croatian elections. Initially the arguments aimed to rewrite the history of relations between the political categories "fascists" and "communists," both of whom had existed all over Yugoslavia's territory. These political terms gradually gave way, however, to the more territorially based *ethnic* terms—"Serb," "Croat," "Slovene," and "Muslim"—as Pamela Ballinger demonstrates for similar conflicts between Slovenes and Italians in the same period.[13] All sides strove to transfigure anonymous skeletons into their own martyrs. Those skeletons then served in the historical revisionism by which new nationalist histories emerged for newly emerging states.

These powerful political symbols entered deeply into public awareness through immense funerals (often televised) for the bones removed from caves. Hayden reports, for example, that in August 1991 there was an immense public funeral in Belgrade for " 'three thousand [Serb] victims of the Ustaša genocide, whose bones were recently removed from ten caves in Herzegovina'" following nine months of exhumations (this was according to Radio Belgrade). "The line of coffins stretched for one and a half kilometers; the liturgy was sung by the patriarch of the Serbian Orthodox Church," with speeches from leading nationalist intellectuals and politicians. A few months later came an exhibition of documentary films about the genocide, seemingly designed "both to demonize Croats as a 'genocidal people' and to stir the passions of Serbs as having been among the great victims of the twentieth century."[14] Such mass events represented the state's having "collectivized" and nationalized the dead bodies hitherto mourned by families as their individual dead.[15] They were part of forming new Serbian, Croatian, and Bosnian nation-states.

So, in a different way, were the smaller, more localized burials that took place in communities all over the new states' territories (see plate 20.[16]). For this task, "nameless" bodies were particularly effective. Because the wartime massacres were so spatially widespread, as has been the fighting during the 1990s, there are literally thousands of possible sites at which dead people might be found and reinterred.[17] In this context, graves laid out a geography of territorial claims and of personal commitment to those claims, for in these places "our" dead were buried. Retrieving and reburying these nameless bones marked the territory

20 Local reburial of people killed in warfare during 1993, hastily buried by their killers, and reburied now with proper rituals. (*Source*: Photo Documentation Archive of *Vreme*, Belgrade)

claimed for a Greater Serbia, one that found its dead in the soil of most of the other republics. We might say that these corpses assisted in reconfiguring space by etching new international borders into it with their newly dug graves.[18]

Led by their vanguards of bones, then, armies of Slovenes, Croats, Serbs, and Muslims proceeded to dismember Yugoslavia, a protracted and potentially endless process in which scarcely does a fragile peace emerge in one area (Bosnia) than conflict erupts in another (Kosovo, Macedonia). In each place, bodies hastily buried by their killers are later dug up and given proper burial. Thus the concern with corpses continues, as the fighting produces ever more graves. Their occupants become grounds for mutual recrimination, objects of deep mourning and of efforts at retrieval for proper burial, and means of a politics of blame, guilt, and accountability. This brief summary condenses all my principal themes for the discussion that follows: the politics of nation-state formation; corpses, space, and territory; grief and proper burial; vengeance and accountability; and revisions of history. All of these are central to reordering postsocialism's worlds of meaning.

RECONFIGURING SPACE

The Politics of Territory

Not surprisingly, nationalist politics goes a long way toward explaining the place of dead bodies in the wars of Yugoslav succession. Aside from manipulations of the dead that spurred nationalist electoral victories, secession, and war, there was the problem of drawing territorial boundaries around the new states. The problem was intractable, given the high intermixture of Serbs, Croats, and Muslims (particularly in Bosnia). According to Susan Woodward, the European Union at first insisted that the borders of Yugoslavia's several republics become the new international borders; the Serbs refused to accept this solution, however, for it would leave about 30 percent of Serbs outside the borders of a new Serbia.[19] From this impasse emerged "ethnic cleansing." It was a response to the European Union's declaring that the border question should be decided by referendum: thus all sides strove to chase "others" off land they hoped to make permanently "theirs." The problem was particularly severe for Serbs. Not only were they more numerous than others outside the borders of their former republic; in Bosnia, they made up nearly three-fourths of the farmers and only a third of the total population. This made land an issue not just of state-making and international diplomacy but also of basic livelihood, and it ruled out any possibility of setting the borders strictly according to population percentages.[20]

The border question became even more unmanageable when combined with some of the matters I raised in chapter 2, concerning global religious realignment and the revitalization of faith. Pope John Paul II's ecumenism extended not only to the patriarch of Constantinople but also to Islam. As became clear at the Cairo conference on population (1996), the pope saw in Islam his best ally on the social issues so important to him. Because in post-Yugoslavia differences of nationality coincide overall with religious difference—Croats are mostly Catholic; Serbs, Orthodox; and many (other[21]) Bosnians, Muslim—the religious competition I discussed in chapter 2 entered into these conflicts, with Orthodox Serbs seeking protection from the Russian patriarch against the pope's Catholic Croats and their Muslim allies.[22] The politics of dead bodies reflects this coincidence of religions with nation-state creation, precisely because the churches hold the ultimate authority with respect to death and burial. Thus religion connects with nation-state borders via (among other things) practices around death. But how can we understand more fully *why* there is this close link between burials and borders? I suggest we think about kinship.

Ancestors, Soil, and Nations

In his classic work *The Ancient City*, Fustel de Coulanges examines Roman, Greek, and other burial practices so as to demonstrate an indissoluble link between localized kinship groups and the land they live on; the link is ancestor worship. Ancestors were buried in the soil around the dwelling; their presence consecrated that soil, and continuous rituals connecting them with their heirs created a single community consisting of the dead, their heirs, and the soil they shared. (Twentieth-century ethnography from Transylvania and Hungary reports additionally that the placenta of a newborn was often buried under the house.[23]) The dead were thought to *live* underground[24] and to require frequent nourishing with food and prayers; in return they gave their descendants protection. A person's death thereby brought him or her into a new social relationship with the living, marked by reciprocal offerings and aid (points I touched on in chapter 1). Comparative ethnography, including that from Transylvania, Slovenia, Croatia, Serbia, and farther east, is full of similar conceptions. It would be easier to dismiss them as marginal if they did not also appear in contemporary ethnography from Western Europe.[25]

I mention these practices not to suggest that nothing has changed since the Romans but to startle readers into thinking differently about nation-states and territory.[26] Such practices remain culturally available for use in new times even if they cease to be widely observed. Indeed, politicians who claim to represent a different, more authentic political order than the one they have overthrown often call for resuming "traditions" like these. Given the close connection between dead people and *soil*, it would be surprising if land-hungry post-Yugoslavs did *not* find such "traditional" practices compelling. I take up this matter below.

To fill out Fustel's argument, I return to the points I made in chapter 1 concerning nationalism as a kind of ancestor worship.[27] There I suggested that nationalisms are forms of ancestor cult, writ large enough to encompass localized kin-group affiliations and to incorporate into the notions of "ancestors," "brothers," and "heirs" people with whom our immediate blood ties are nil. On this reading, to rebury a dead person is not simply to reassess his place in history;[28] it is to revise national genealogies, inserting the person as an ancestor more centrally into the lineage of honored forebears. Thus ideas about kinship are highly relevant to modern-day politics. This is especially true of post-Yugoslavia, where kinship structures are highly salient in social life and intergroup relations.[29] (In saying this, I do not mean to call Yugoslavia a "tribal" or "primitive" place, *pace* widespread media commentary to that effect, but to say only that the process of state-building in this region continually shored up the existence of supranuclear family groupings. What state-building accomplished was largely to supplement an emphasis on lineal ancestry with that of blood brotherhood, as a metaphor for nationhood.[30])

To illustrate political use of this nationalism-kinship connection, I quote from the inflammatory 1987 speech that catapulted Slobodan Milošević straight into the leadership of Serbia. Visiting Kosovo province[31] to attend to the complaints of Serbs who reside among Albanians there, he baptized a new Serb nationalist politics with these words, aimed at convincing the dissatisfied Serbs to remain in Kosovo rather than leave:

> You should stay here. This is your land. These are your houses. Your memories. You shouldn't abandon your land. It was never part of the Serbian character to give up in the face of obstacles. You should stay here for the sake of your ancestors and descendants. Otherwise your ancestors would be defiled and descendants disappointed. But I don't suggest that you should stay, endure, and tolerate a situation you're not satisfied with. On the contrary, you should change it.[32]

Note that leaving the land would mean *defiling* the ancestors, and recall those Bosnian Serbs who took their ancestors *with* them. The mass reaction to this speech showed Milošević that he had hit upon a perfect political formula: articulating Serb national sentiment through references to *kinship rooted in particular soils.*

The connection among kinship, burial, nationalism, and soil is a very potent and widespread one. We find it illustrated in fiction: for example,

Günter Grass's novel *The Call of the Toad* shows people trying to create a Polish-German reconciliation by allowing Germans expelled from Gdansk in 1945 to be (re)buried there; Polish nationalists scuttle the plan, protesting that the German corpses would recolonize Polish soil.[33] Second, and very appropriately, the same cluster of themes—proper and improper burial, mobile dead, descent groups, and soils that have a national quality—are at the heart of Bram Stoker's famous *Dracula*. In his rendition, Dracula must go to London *in his own soil*, shipped in numerous coffins.[34] In England he sets about creating new lineages of offspring by sucking English blood, thereby annexing English territory and endangering England's integrity as a nation, for the new vampirelings will sleep by day in *their* own (English) soil.[35] Given that the best way to kill a vampire is to drive a stake through its heart and (a crucial detail) *into the earth beneath*, so as to hold it securely in its grave,[36] perhaps here is a creative inversion of the idea that proper burial, of the kind that permits an orderly universe and fruitful relations with kin and ancestors, must occur in *one's own (national?) soil*.

The kinship-soil-nationalism connection is powerful not just fictionally but also politically. Examples include the Tomb of the Unknown Soldier in Moscow, which is surrounded by six marble blocks containing sacred earth from each of six "hero cities"; this earth was drenched with the blood of brave soldiers in World War II.[37] The same principle appears in the 1894 funeral of Hungary's 1848 revolutionary hero, Lajos Kossuth. According to Martha Lampland, plans for it included bringing lumps of soil to Budapest from every site where the blood of Hungarian patriots had been shed in 1848, and mixing these lumps with the soil from Kossuth's grave. The plan was later expanded to include soil from other important national sites as well.[38]

Connections of this kind suggest ways of assigning new values to space (reconfiguring it), the larger point with which I opened this section. If we look at relations between ancestors and the idea of proper burial, I believe we grasp the place of dead-body politics in nation-state formation even more fully.

ANCESTORS AND PROPER BURIAL

For those who take ancestors seriously (and I think there is more of this around than one might imagine), the politics of reburial engages the abiding sociality of relations between living and dead. As I suggested in chapter 1, these relations include not just mourning loved ones but also fearing them, as sources of possible harm; one must therefore closely observe the myriad rules and requirements of proper burial, for they affect the relations of both living and dead to the world that all inhabit.[39] Because my ethnographic information about Yugoslav burial practices is not extensive, I must be modest in my claims for the points I am about to make, which are drawn not only from post-Yugoslavia but also from Transylvania, Hungary, and Ukraine, concerning beliefs thought to be more general to this region.[40]

As in those other places, proper care of the dead is a matter of great concern in the former Yugoslavia.[41] Communist Milovan Djilas even explains in these terms Montenegrin peasants' World War II support of the Četniks against the communist partisans they had favored at first. The communists, says Djilas, mistreated dead bodies, hurling them into ravines ("less for convenience than to avoid the funeral processions and the inconsolable and fearless mourners"); the Četniks, by contrast, treated the dead with respect, retrieving corpses from the ravines and giving them solemn burial.[42] Post-Yugoslavs (most especially Serbs) hold strong ideas about proper burial and about continuing relations with dead kin. Weekly visits to tombs and frequent commemorations are the norm. In chapter 1 I observed that mortuary hospitality had intensified in Serbia beginning in the 1970s, as villagers built entire houses on the graves of their kin within which to hold ongoing relations of visiting and feasting. The same principle of concern for the dead is apparent also in its obverse: violence against enemy graves. This practice has a history at least as old as World War II, as Pamela Ballinger found in her research on the flight of Italians from territory given over to Yugoslavia: the new Slovene masters made a point of defacing Italian tombstones, writing Slavic names over the Italian ones and removing the corpses.[43] Such practices were echoed in the wars of the 1990s, as Serbs machine-gunned the contents of Croat graves.[44]

I would like to make two points about proper burial and post-Yugoslav politics. The first has to do with proper burial and community-making, the second with burial and land claims. For both, my argument is that ideas central to cosmic reordering—such as the idea that cosmic order comes from right relations of kin, including proper interment—can work not just cognitively but also politically. Their political effects permit us to think about these "traditional" ideas without presupposing that they have unbroken continuity from past times.

Burials and reburials serve both to create and to reorder community. They do so in part simply by bringing live people together to eat, drink, gossip, and exchange gifts and information, and in part by setting up exchanges (usually of food and objects) with the dead, whom they thereby bring as ancestors into a single community with them. Beyond these effects, as Robert Hertz argued, (re)burials reaffirm the political community of those who orient to them.[45] I suggest that in the post-Yugoslav context they serve not just to *reaffirm* community but also to *narrow* and *bound* it.[46] A (re)burial creates an audience of "mourners," all of whom think they have some relation to the dead person. The question is, *Which* aggregate of people is brought together (directly or indirectly) for this event? Whom does the gathering of mourners leave out who might have been present a year or two ago? For political reburials, this becomes, Who is to be included in or excluded from the new national society that is being made? Thus post-Yugoslav reburials create new, narrower, national communities, as the group of participants has come to be monoethnic. Whereas Bosnia's Muslims used to go to the burials of their Serb or Croat covillagers and vice versa, for instance, that is no longer possible.[47] Burials bring people together, reminding them of the reason for their collective presence—relatedness—but that relatedness has now become ethnically exclusive.

Hertz saw a homology between the communities of living and dead. Expanding upon his logic, I suggest that reorganizing relations with the dead can be a way of reordering live human communities. That is, precisely because the human community includes both living and dead, any manipulation of the dead automatically affects relations with and among the living. This is what post-Yugoslav corpse politics does. Acknowledging certain people as ancestors and kin, and gathering a specific living public to rectify relations with the community of the dead through proper burial, reorganize relations among the living. I prefigured this argument in chapter 2, where I observed that Inochentie Micu's reburial created a community of chiefly *Greek Catholic* mourners, rather than the much larger community (including Orthodox) that might have been created by commemorating him strictly as a *national* hero. Similarly with Hungarian Imre Nagy, of chapter 1: because Communist Party participation in his reburial was expressly limited, the event created a much larger community—all Hungarians who had suffered under the previous regime—and inscribed Nagy in the very long list of nationalist freedom fighters. Thus concerning the mass burial service in Belgrade in 1991 mentioned above, with a procession of coffins a kilometer and a half long, I can now observe that the mourners were, emphatically, Serbs burying Serbs as their national kin. In brief, I suggest that postsocialist reburials involve reconfiguring human communities according to new standards of inclusion and exclusion.

My second point concerns proper burial and land claims, which bring us back to the theme of reconfiguring space. In discussing the links among ancestors, soil, and nations, I noted that such conceptions make kinsmen, descendants, territory, and specific burial sites inseparable from each other. Attachment to the burial sites of kin poses major problems for redrawing nation-state borders, however, for its obvious corollary is that people should not move from the places where their kin are buried. If they do, then they lose their social bearings—unless they take their kin along or maintain contact with them in other ways.

Consider in this light some fragmentary evidence from Serbia, Croatia, and Bosnia concerning present-day attachment to kin and the soil of their burial.[48] In February 1996, following the Dayton accords, five Sarajevo suburbs were to be transferred from the control of Serbs to that of the Muslims they had expelled during the fighting. NATO and the Office of the High Representative (OHR) botched the job, Muslim gangs began looting and murdering Serbs, and the Serbs decided to leave. Before departing, they dug up the graves of their kin (these Serbs had been living there for generations) and took the contents with them.[49] As the head grave digger in one cemetery told a reporter, "People say they cannot live without being able to come to the grave every Sunday to light a candle and put down flowers."[50] This transport occasioned great expense, since huge fees were levied for transferring bodies "across state lines." Imposing such "customs duty" clearly demarcated "our" buriable soil from "theirs" (offering the perfect contrast with the duty-free trip of Frederick the Great from West to East Germany, mentioned in the introduction).

Muslims and Croats had the same concern but were prepared to travel for it, rather than take ancestral bones along with them. A main demand of Muslims following the Dayton accords was that they be allowed to return home so they could tend the graves of their dead. Likewise, in ongoing UN-mediated talks about territories that Croats were being asked to cede, a critical issue was the demand of Croats displaced from those territories to be able to cross the new border to visit their dead whenever they wished, most particularly on All Souls' Day.

I am not going to challenge whether those who use this idiom of proper burial are indeed attached to ancestral graves; I assume that many of them are. It is worth noting, nevertheless, that the idiom buttresses certain kinds of land claims. The same could be said of Istrian exiles' self-construction as deeply wronged by having had to leave their dead in Istria, improperly mourned.[51] Perhaps Muslims and Croats, in holding out for visits to tend their kinsmen's graves, are simply craftier than Serbs, who, in taking their dead along, leave no grounds for claiming access to the former burial place. In other words, Muslims and Croats may be acting from strategic calculation rather than from mortuary custom: they want an excuse to go back. Whether or not their sentiments are genuine or calculated is, however, unimportant for my purposes. What counts is that their calculations use an idiom—in fact a very old one—linking people with the geographical emplacement of their dead, and this idiom is both culturally and politically powerful.

I consider these examples additional support for my view that grave sites, ancestors, and nation-state formation are interconnected. Exhuming and reburying (or at least going to visit) the bodies of kin enriches the meanings both of the human communities that assemble there and of the soil itself.[52] These actions thereby reconfigure space and, in at least two ways, give it new significances apt for creating new nation-states. First, they saturate countless spaces with powerful emotion that blends the personal grief of kin with rage against the enemy, nationally conceived.[53] Second, they lay out a geography of territorial claims pertinent to drawing new international borders. Thus burying or reburying ancestors and kin sacralizes and nationalizes spaces as "ours," binding people to their national territories in an orderly universe.

RECONFIGURING TIME

Accountability and the Past: Rewriting History

I suggested above that reburials narrow and bound the community of mourners, excluding persons no longer welcome in the national kin group of the new nation-state. These effects come not just from who participates in which reburials but also from controversies over *culpability* and *accountability*: Who is responsible for these deaths, and how should the guilty be brought to justice? Part of a seemingly worldwide phenomenon of seeking retribution and holding people accountable for past wrongs (think of Argentina, Guatemala, and, in a quite different way, South Africa),[54] these widespread processes aim at social and political reconciliation—at "settling accounts," in Borneman's words.[55] As I observed in chapter 1, post-socialist blaming and retribution-seeking are part of reordering morality, making the new order a moral one in contrast with the old (for at least some people). Pursuing accountability and justice around dead bodies in these cases also serves to reconfigure time by rewriting history. I will begin illustrating this point with post-Yugoslav examples and will then broaden my discussion into a more general treatment of reconfiguring time.

In post-Yugoslavia, dead bodies have been a principal means of blaming and demanding accountability. It was the discovery of mass burials in caves that began Croat-Serb contests over who was to blame for which set of massacres. Presidents Tudjman and Milošević, by taking up the matter on behalf of the presumed Croat and Serb victims, sought to augment the moral authority of their respective governments. The process involved much more, however, than establishing blame: it involved creating certain kinds of social actors. To determine accountability necessarily entails identifying the guilty and the victims. *Which* kind of social being can be effectively blamed and held accountable? The state? The former regime? An ethnic or national group? Single individuals? One means for settling accounts has been lustration laws, such as those in the Czech Republic and Poland, which hold the prior regime collectively responsible but single out individuals for punishment.[56] Other governments, such as Romania's and Bulgaria's, resisted making such laws, reasoning that because so many people were complicit, *none* would be blameless, and to punish a former regime is impossible.

What distinguishes these cases from the post-Yugoslav ones is that whereas in the former the guilty collective actor is a political organization—the Communist Party—in the latter the culpable collective actors are not political entities but ethnonational ones. Initial discoveries of Serb and Croat mass graves presented their contents as the victims of "Ustaša," "communists," and "Četniks"; soon, however, the perpetrators changed to "Croats" and "Serbs." Thus responsibility for the previous crimes of political organizations slid onto the shoulders of ethnonational groups. Pamela Ballinger shows precisely this process in accountability demands over the mass graves of Slovenes and Italians in the Julian March.[57] Because reciprocal accusations of genocide were flung at *groups*, not individuals, and responsibility was attributed to collective actors, retribution took the form of collective punishment through new massacres. There is a stark contrast between these ideas of accountability and those pursued by the Hague War Crimes Tribunal, whose goal is to identify culpable *individuals* and try them with evidence from specific individual victims.[58]

These questions of moral responsibility are questions not merely of recompense in the present, however, but also of revising the past. Dead-body politics involving accountability and justice connects with my earlier observations about ancestors, reburials, and national community-making, through the theme of rewriting history. Commentators who have written on this topic generally agree that the politics of corpses is about reorienting people's relations to the past.[59] Who are our true ancestors? Who has been unjustly shunted aside, and who has usurped their place in our lineal self-definition?—that is, about what set of people will our national history be rewritten? (Ambulant statues and corpses figure prominently in these matters.) Which ancestors will our history acknowledge, which forget? Some of this work of rewriting (or of creating histories for new nation-states) may occur through the bones of the nameless, and some through famous heroes whose place in genealogies a reburial rediscovers.

Throughout the postsocialist world there has been a veritable orgy of historical revisionism, of writing the communist period out of the past; corpse politics is central to it.[60] We make better sense of that process if we see it as a reaction to the equally thoroughgoing historical revisionism attempted by the various communist parties during their rule. The multiple ways in which they revised histories included all the usual practices:

bringing into history books previously unremarked persons or events that might be seen to prefigure the communist social transformation (a 1933 workers' strike, an early socialist thinker), or recasting the images of persons and events already in the textbooks; suppressing names and dates whose mention might induce inappropriate associations, thus turning them into nonpersons and nonevents; airbrushing out of photographs anyone who fell from favor;[61] and placing the regime's many nameless victims in unmarked graves. Such practices were to fortify Communist Party rule. Rév writes: "As long as the graves remained unmarked, the victims unnamed, the prosecutors could suppose that they ruled the company of the hanged."[62]

Against this backdrop, the orgy of historical revisionism since 1989 is seen as a rectification of communist censorship and lies. The large majority of repatriations and reburials since 1989 have been of people who, during the communist period, fled or were exiled from their home countries and could not be or did not want to be buried there (such as Hungary's Bartók and Poland's Sikorsky); people whom the communists had persecuted or killed (such as László Rajk and Imre Nagy, in Hungary; Rudolf Slánský, in Czechoslovakia; or the family of the tsar, in Russia); people whose histories the communists had suppressed (such as the nameless dead in Ukrainian forests or Yugoslav caves, and the famous men of the fascist period); and so on. The people whom the communists airbrushed out are particularly apt symbols for deleting the communist era itself from the new histories, thus signifying its death. Reburials accomplish this by revisiting the bodies of persons the communists mistreated, resurrecting them, and placing them in a new light.[63]

But the communist practices pose difficulties for subsequent revisions: If everyone already knows that history can be manipulated, then how can the authorities now produce a truth effect?[64] Dead bodies are particularly helpful in resolving this problem. Manipulating physical remains is a visual and visceral experience that seems to offer true access to the past. I suggested earlier that corpses are effective symbols because they are protean while being concrete; here it is their *concreteness* that I wish to emphasize. If one wants to revise the past in the age of virtual reality, when people can indeed be airbrushed out of or technologically inserted into history, it is comforting to have actual bones in hand. (This does not guarantee, of course, that those bones "really belong" to the dead person in question.[65])

Perhaps this point illuminates a marvelous episode reported by journalist Tim Judah, when Tito "came back" for two days in 1994. As a joke, Belgrade's radio station B-92 hired an actor, dressed him up as Tito, and followed him around to record people's reactions to him. Astonishingly, people reacted as if it were the real Tito, come back to life. They would stop to blame him for things he had done wrong, accuse him of being pro-American, complain about present problems and his role in producing them, or express their nostalgia for the days when he ruled Yugoslavia. The deputy director of B-92 observed of the prank, "It shows that the common people have lost touch with reality. Everything you tell them through the media they absorb like a sponge. So you have a situation where Tito is resurrected and people believe that."[66] I think, rather, that amid all the confusion, lies, and illusions that were permeating daily life in Belgrade, Tito's seemingly palpable body created a truth effect stronger than widespread common knowledge of his death. (Even the *New York Times* appears to recognize Tito's transcendent properties: on December 2, 1997, it carried a headline, "Though Still Dead, Tito Can Be Reached on Line."[67])

These observations raise once again the matter of dead bodies and sentiment. The emotional force of reburials that arouse sentiments related to death is undoubtable in the case of reburials of our own beloved, dead within memory—that is, in cases like Yugoslavia—whose departure leaves us feeling amputated long after the fact, for our life with those immediate dead has formed us as persons. But, as I suggested for Inochentie Micu, even public reburials of famous people who were not our friends and kin awaken complex emotions, wherever genealogies have been so successfully integrated into national imagery that people view the famous dead as in some sense also "ours." Relevant here are my earlier remarks about East European national ideologies and victimization, closely tied to questions of blame and accountability. Like saints, ancestors engage deep feeling when their biographies can be cast in that most common of all nationalist tropes: suffering. The revival of religion has intensified this imagery. When it can be said of a dead person that, like Christ, he suffered—for the faith, for the nation, for the cause—then that gives his corpse both sanctity and a basis for empathic identification. The reason is not just that many people in Eastern Europe are currently suffering, but that national ideologies there have so successfully crafted an identification between personal suffering and the suffering of one's nation.

What am I claiming in the above discussion? I have pointed to a number of themes (proper burial, reconfiguring time and space, culpability, and so on) concerning the use of dead bodies in revising history. Sometimes these themes rest on a substrate of popular belief, sometimes they are manipulated for political effect. Touching as they do on matters of accountability, justice, personal grief, victimization, and suffering, dead bodies as vehicles of historical revision are freighted with strong emotion. To the extent that they have been politically effective, one reason is the associations they evoke for people whose feelings of disorientation make them receptive to arguments, stories, and symbols that seem to give them a compass. In post-Yugoslavia the terrible displacements of persons, the tortures and murders, the devastating inflation, and so on surely indicate that the cosmos is out of joint.[68] Among the things people know of that produce such misery are the vengeful souls of the improperly buried and of ancestral spirits inadequately tended. Without claiming that this interpretation "explains" what is happening in Yugoslavia, I believe these ideas deepen our comprehension of its dead-body politics by exploring matters of affect. (Their relevance to other cases remains, of course, an open question.[69])

Time Compression and the Shapes of History

And so reburials revise the past by returning names to the nameless and perhaps endowing these revisions with feeling. Such outcomes are common to dead-body politics everywhere. I believe, however, that in the postsocialist world there is more to it than that. History is not simply being rewritten with new/old characters and a different plot line—for instance, a plot that replaces the communist radiant future with a narrative of tyranny overthrown and resistance triumphant. Rather, the very notions of time that underlie history are thrown open to question. By this I mean that several different things are potentially altered: the *understanding of temporal process* that enables people to excise the socialist period in their revisions of history; the *shapes of history* (often unconscious) in terms of which people act; and the *conception of time's passage* implicit in their actions. Changes in any of these amount to "reconfiguring time."

Writing of the Nagy reburial, István Rév helps us to discern the first of these three possibilities while also tying it to the topics of accountability and justice:

> Retroactive political justice brings the past closer to the present. The embarrassing times can thus be erased by turning them into *Jetztzeit*. By changing the length of eclipsed time, history is shortened. The replay of the sins brings certain episodes of the past nearer, and can help in compressing time. By bringing back and reburying the repressed, the time between the [first] burial and the final funeral is put into brackets. A new chronology is created by the immediatization of the remote.[70]

This observation is crucial, for it shows that the reburial did not just reevaluate the events of 1956 but reconfigured time itself. Rév points to two important elements of Imre Nagy's reburial in Heroes' Square: on the right side of the square was the Yugoslav embassy, in which Nagy had sought asylum when Soviet troops entered Budapest in November 1956; meanwhile, loudspeakers broadcast Nagy's last words to his executioners, *in his own voice*. It was as if this huge commemoration were following his execution, which had just happened. The intervening thirty-odd years had simply vanished.

Many postsocialist historical revisions have proceeded in exactly this way, although usually with reference to the mid-1940s rather than Nagy's 1956: they join the precommunist period directly to the 1990s. This practice reveals an interesting conception of time, in which time is not fixed and irreversible. One can pick up the time line, snip out and discard the communist piece of it that one no longer wishes to acknowledge, paste the severed ends together, and hey presto! one has a new historical time line. One has not accepted and incorporated the recent past, one has simply excised it. Excising the communist period often occurs by treating it as an aberration; throughout the former socialist bloc one hears repeatedly that what everyone wants now is to repossess a "normal" past and weave it into "normal" presents and futures.[71] This conception is evident in every rehabilitation of a cultural or political personage from World War II, in every attempt to extirpate "communism" from people's lives and to demand compensation for the wrongs it wrought, and in every call for a *restitutio in integrum* of the status quo ante (a primary means being the return of properties to those who had them before).

Facilitating excision of the communist period is the shallowness of Bolshevism's own historical roots. It dated itself largely from the mid-nineteenth century (the writings of Marx and Engels), emphasizing its own novelty and its supersession of local histories heretofore, and its end in a radically different future. It strove to suppress Christian temporalities and replace them with festivals and rhythms of its own.[72] Having a short time line also means having a shallow genealogy: Bolshevism's founding ancestors lie only four generations back, a flash in the pan compared with the minimum of seven generations any male Serb could recount to ethnographer Eugene Hammel in the 1960s.[73] Indeed, the communist time line, with its emphasis on breaking from the past toward a radically different future, militates against having many ancestors. The collapse of Communist Party rule opens the door to those other temporalities of Christianity and of kinship affiliation—both of which yield much broader and deeper pasts than anything the communists could muster.[74] Using these deeper temporalities, postsocialist politicians can present themselves (sometimes by manipulating dead bodies) as heirs to a precommunist past.

Thus the present rewriting of history is about far more than making a new story: what is at stake is the very *shape* of history. Different conceptions of human action in the past have different shapes (shallow or deep, broad or narrow). These shapes, in turn, enter into people's life experiences: because the sense of self rests partly on a sense of *being-in-time*, the shape people attribute to history infuses both individuals' and groups' self-understanding. Therefore, locating oneself in time is a function of the shape one accords it. We can grasp this idea best by considering the shape of history inherent in various ideas about kinship.

History has a different shape, depending on what notions of ancestry and genealogy prevail; figure 1 illustrates some shapes of history according to different notions of ancestry.[75] Where people in the present think of the world as inhabited by themselves and their fellows, all descended from an "eponymous ancestor" in the deep past, history takes on the shape of a cone or pyramid (figure 1a). By contrast, where people in the present think of the world as inhabited by individuals like themselves, each the product of many forefathers, the cone is inverted into a fan (figure 1b). Then there are the knotty clusters characteristic of bilateral kinship systems (figure 1c), in which ego counts as relatives (1) his/her parents and grandparents but rarely more distant forebears; (2) his/her own siblings plus their spouses; (3) his/her children and siblings' children; (4) perhaps the siblings and children of own and parents' cousins; and (5) his/her grandchildren. The result includes both short cones and short fans and resembles the most common kinship system in the United States. In that kind of system one situates oneself in a fairly shallow time line and one's sense of self is more present-oriented than in lineal systems, in which the cones and beads of relatedness can be very deep. A shallow time line often accompanies a strong sense of individual agency in the present moment, while a deeper one favors, instead, a potentially drawn-out and collective sense of agency. These differences are crucial elements of personal and group self-understanding.

Kinship systems characteristically exclude some people who might be counted in, while including others. For example, Old Testament genealogies take the shape of a string of beads, with a central line of "begats" running from Adam through a long line of patriarchs on to the anticipated Messiah (New Testament ones continue on to a second Messiah as well); they leave out ancillary lines and women. Because the underlying system is patrilineal, its dominant imagery is cone-shaped (descendants of a common ancestor), although, depending on one's purposes, one might emphasize the entire lineage (the cone) or just the patriline (the string of begats) (figure 1d). Similarly, in traditional China one's sense of whom one is related to across an extended time looks like a rake, with a line of firstborn male ancestors forming the rake's handle, the offspring of the present heir's grandfather or great-grandfather being its teeth (offspring of female consanguines would not appear in this rake but in that of their husbands) (figure 1e).[76] The genealogy of communism is a foreshortened version of this rake: it has a vertical handle of three "begats"—Marx begat Lenin begat Stalin—followed by a quick radiation outward of "offspring," in the Party heads of the various satellite countries (figure 1). Here we see a historical shape that resembles that of a kinship system, though it substitutes political kinship for blood links. It is possible to imagine intermeshing rakes, in which certain unrelated persons (three, as in figure 1g) are taken to be ancestors of today's larger kin group.

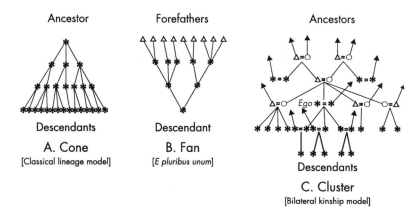

Ancestor

A. Cone
[Classical lineage model]

Forefathers

Descendant

B. Fan
[E pluribus unum]

Ancestors

Descendants

C. Cluster
[Bilateral kinship model]

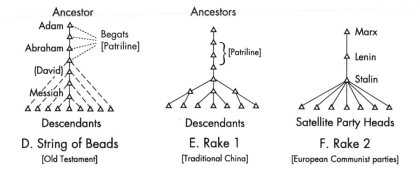

Ancestor

Adam
Abraham
(David)
Messiah

Begats
[Patriline]

Descendants

D. String of Beads
[Old Testament]

Ancestors

[Patriline]

Descendants

E. Rake 1
[Traditional China]

Marx
Lenin
Stalin

Satellite Party Heads

F. Rake 2
[European Communist parties]

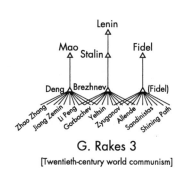

Lenin

Mao
Stalin
Fidel

Deng
Brezhnev
(Fidel)

Zhao Zhang
Jiang Zemin
Li Peng
Gorbachev
Yeltsin
Zyuganov
Allende
Sandinistas
Shining Path

G. Rakes 3
[Twentieth-century world communism]

△ MALE   ○ FEMALE   ✳ SEX IRRELEVANT   = MARRIAGE | DESCENT

FIGURE I Some Shapes of Genealogical History

These thoughts bear on locating oneself not only in a specific kinship system but also, through the argument I made earlier, in one's *nation* as kinship writ large. National kinship imageries are not fixed but vary; they, too, include some kinds of "brothers" and exclude others, and the resulting imageries produce communities with particular shapes in time. How one feels about oneself as part of the national family will vary accordingly. Thinking about history's different shapes relative to how different kinship organizations lay out relatedness in time enables us to see how nation as kindred might serve as more than simply a metaphor.

Reconfigured Temporalities and Alternative Political Projects

I have been speaking so far of the implications of history's shapes for how people situate themselves socially and in time, providing fundamental elements of their identity. To conclude this section I would like to expand these remarks to include conceptions of temporality itself: how people understand (and, by their actions, create) what "time" is. I do not plan to treat this subject comprehensively but only to offer a few reflections.

In his influential essay on time,[77] Edmund Leach wrote that the two most basic temporalities are the linear and the cyclical: time is perceived either as moving in a straight line (our common notion of "progress," for instance) or as doubling back on itself in circles (a common conception among populations whose lives are governed by the agricultural cycle). Linear time may be slanted upward (reflecting progress) or not (showing simple social reproduction, or even decay); cyclical time, likewise (showing a long-term upward trend, as in cycles of capital accumulation, or not). Again, time may be thought of as continuous and even infinite, having no beginning or end; or it may be discontinuous, with cataclysmic beginnings (the Creation, the Bolshevik Revolution, the "Big Bang" of present-day astronomers) or endings (the Last Judgment of some Christian conceptions, the "death of the nation" feared by nationalists). Figure 2 illustrates some of the possibilities.

Temporal conceptions are crucial elements of human experience. They ground it by establishing the largely unconscious expectations within which people live out their lives.[78] Furthermore, as Erik Mueggler has shown in a brilliant essay on time and agency in China, different temporal

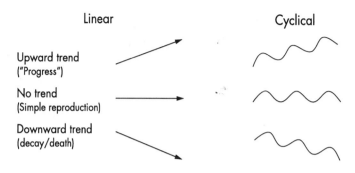

A. Forms of Temporal Movement

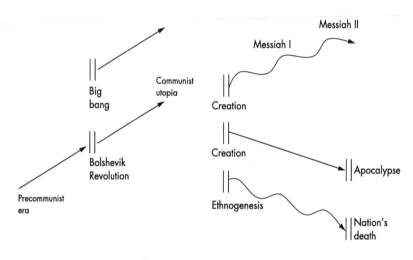

B. Forms of Discontinuity (indicated by ⏸)

FIGURE 2 Conceptions of Time

conceptions may accompany great differences in how human agency is understood.[79] That, in turn, has implications for the matter of accountability, which I mentioned above: whether the accountable action is seen to be the responsibility of autonomous individual subjects, of ghosts, or of collective actors will affect decisions about punishment or compensation.

No human group has one and only one conception of time, uniformly experienced by all, although one temporal conception may be societally dominant. For example, the temporality privileged in Western industrial societies is primarily linear and directed upward, resting on a central notion of endless progress; within this, one may find groups with different experiences (such as homeless people or minorities)[80] and conceptions (an apocalyptic end of time, a Judeo-Christian cyclicity from the first Messiah to the Second Coming, and so on). Communist planning similarly assumed linear progress but posited an effectively timeless end state that would be the communist utopia; the imagery was of a socialist road to the future. Actual experience within "planned" economies was otherwise, however, as poor coordination gave rise to spastic work rhythms of speedup (the celebrated "storming") and standstill (recall the Hungarian film *Time Stands Still*).[81]

Among the more unsettling aspects of postsocialist transformation, I believe, is the possibility that the temporal experiences and conceptions familiar to people during the socialist period are being changed, especially for elites. Intellectual and political elites feel themselves caught in a terrible time bind, for example; many complain that the pace of their lives has become dizzying and almost unbearable, compared with before.[82] They face, in other words, a potential reconfiguring of how time is conceived and lived. There are several reasons why, and means through which, this might be happening. One means is political struggle over competing political agendas, as social actors pursue projects whose implicit temporalities differ. From the altered balance of political forces after the collapse of Soviet-style socialism emerged a political free-for-all. Among the many contending groups were religious elites (as in chapter 2), nationalists (chapters 1–3), neoliberals (chapter 1), neocommunists, and so on. Implicit in their programs were different temporal conceptions, which their strife brought into conflict. In struggles over property, understandings of the political process, ideas about blame and punishment, representations of the future, and all manner of other political issues, one can find different groups acting within the frame of different temporalities.

For example, nationalist politicians have a number of temporal options as well as varying potential allies. Some operate within a cyclical time sense, governed by the life-cycle metaphor of birth, growth, decay, and death. Their worst fear is the possibility that their nation might die, a prospect they may see as more urgent than economic crisis. For them, dead bodies—especially of national heroes—are politically vital in showing that because a dead person has posthumous life, the nation itself need not fear death. Anxiety about national death has consequences for the policies of these "cyclical nationalists." They will give high priority to promoting the nation's biological and social reproduction, through antiabortion policies and restrictions on minority-language education for those of other nationalities, for example. Fear of national death may also govern policy in other ways, as in Eduard Beneš's decisions not to take Czechoslovakia into war in 1938 or 1948, decisions he justified explicitly in terms of national death.[83]

Cyclical nationalists may find themselves drawn into alliance with religious elites whose time horizon is very long, absorbing cycles of religious persecution and revival while preserving the people's faith toward the Last Judgment. (Thus I find it no accident that Mančevsky's celebrated film *Before the Rain* is structured around a cyclical temporality of national conflict that intersects in the figure of an Orthodox priest.) In Romania this kind of alliance appeared between cyclical nationalists and the Romanian Orthodox Church, renowned for taking the long view—hence its justification for collaborating with the Communist Party, a small price to pay for not being altogether suppressed. The Romanian case is further complicated, however, by property questions and a religious "market" that compel the church to take action within an unusually short time frame.

In contrast to cyclical nationalists are more "linear" ones who see the nation's fate as wrapped up more with its economic viability than with its demography. These groups might find allies among reform politicians concerned with the fate of the economy, including neoliberals and market-oriented neocommunists. In cases such as Hungary, where the 1994 elections brought a neoliberal/neocommunist coalition, no concessions need be made to the nationalists; but in other cases (such as Poland, perhaps) a possible alliance with "linear nationalists" might require compromise, if for various reasons the nationalists prefer a gradualist approach to reform instead of "shock therapy." Indeed, in those famous alternatives we see how essential temporalities are in pursuing different policy options. Because neoliberals are likely to have a more compressed and urgent sense of time's passage than are neocommunists, the former may find themselves supporting Protestants or Greek Catholics over Orthodox in struggles over property, as in the case of Romania. Within each postsocialist country, the alternative policies and alliances will produce arrays of temporalities that differ from case to case.

These points have practical implications for outside involvement as well. Western politicians and investors see their best local allies as those who seem to have "put the [communist] past behind them" (presupposing a progressive linear time sense). If outsiders overlook the temporal nuances, however, they may find themselves misled. As I noted above, revising history in Eastern Europe often means snipping out and discarding sections of the time line, then attaching the precommunist period to the present and future as the country's true or authentic trajectory and thus putting the communist past behind them. That result emerges, however, from not one but two different temporalities. Those snipping out the socialist period on a time line that is linear do not necessarily repudiate socialism's equally linear orientation; they merely see the linear trajectory it adopted as somehow off (maybe aiming too high or too far to the left), or its rate of progress as too slow.[84] The snipping out thus rectifies an unnecessary detour. For actors whose time sense is more cyclical, by contrast, that same snipping out comes from excising a full temporal cycle, not simply modifying an initial angle of departure. When such groups join the ends of the truncated time line, they are by no means redirecting it progressively. Each of these scenarios comes with a different set of future policy options. Therefore, Western policymakers seeking evidence that one political group or another is "progressive" and "anticommunist" should be careful of interpreting any and all excisions of the communist past as a sure sign of reformist intent.

In sum, the politics and revisions of history occurring around dead bodies participate in an epochal kind of time shift, from which may issue new paradigms for thinking about time and the future. Here we have "reconfiguring time" in its broadest sense. The new organizations of time that will emerge depend on which political forces become allied and perhaps dominant. If, in the long term, political struggles settle into a pattern of alternating parties or coalitions, a certain temporality may become hegemonic—and, with it, certain time disciplines and the economic patterns associated with them.

CONCLUSION

Our space is finite and our time linear; let me bring this book to a close. In doing so, I revisit a thought posed early in the book and again at the start of this chapter. It concerns the relation between the substance of my arguments in the book and the different forms taken by chapters 2 and 3. I hope that the way I presented my discussion of shifting temporalities has helped readers to sense how disorienting and complicated are the transformations brought about in postsocialism. In this chapter, by repeatedly returning to and interweaving the numerous themes of earlier chapters—accountability and compensation, emotion, morality, kinship and ancestors, national identities, space and soil, revising history, and so on—I have tried to do two things. One is to use the chapter's very form (recursive) in contrast with that of chapter 2 (linear), so as to insinuate my argument about temporality into readers' unsuspecting imaginations. The second is to illustrate the magnitude, richness, and complexity of the issues at the heart of postsocialist transformation. In these ways I have sought to show how arresting, even enchanted, the study of postsocialist politics might be, compared with standard fare in this literature.

I have done so by emphasizing political symbolism and questions of meaning. Using dead bodies as my subject(s) has facilitated showing how the very multiplicity of available meanings makes something (such as a dead body) a good political symbol, effective in moments of system transformation. It has also facilitated a complex argument about the place of "tradition" in contemporary politics. Symbols come with histories, but they are used in contexts that modify them. Ideas about ancestry in contemporary nationalism or the mortuary beliefs underlying today's reburials are not "the same" as those of a few decades ago. They provide present-day social actors with ways of talking about the past and of integrating into present action possible "traditions" whose most important role may be to signify the rejection of the "aberrant" communist period and a return to an ostensibly more authentic national history. Furthermore, these kinds of ideas and practices participate in the cosmic domain, a domain political analysis too often ignores and one to which dead bodies afford special access. Cosmic concerns and reordering universes of meaning, I have suggested, are essential to the transformations of postsocialism; if nothing else, they provide the material for symbolizing a new (cosmic) order even if in several respects what is emerging resembles the socialist one.

Although I illustrate my themes with postsocialist cases, I believe my demonstration has consequences beyond them. The reason is the argument with which I began chapter 1: that the transformation of socialism is not an isolated occurrence but part of a wider process of global change. The matters I have pursued here are not limited to Eastern Europe and the former Soviet Union but appear elsewhere as well. Worldwide, we find struggles over property (especially *intellectual* property rights, involving indigenous peoples); questions of accountability and responsibility (as in South Africa); a crisis within many societies as to what "morality" means (the United States is an excellent example); continued national conflicts and the possible reconfiguring of national groups even in "advanced" countries (Quebecois separatism in Canada, Welsh and Scottish parliamentary devolution in the British Isles); crises in political authority (including the various scandals over campaign financing and other matters during the Clinton administration); wholly altered experiences of space and time (by use of the Internet and through the "time-space compression" that accompanies the shift to flexible accumulation[85]); an animation of religious activity in many parts of the world (sometimes mixed with identity politics, as in the Hindu and Sikh conflicts in India); and so on.

To think usefully about the politics bound up with these signs of epochal shift requires, it seems to me, a richer and more meaningful conception of what politics itself consists of. We might call it a more enchanted view of politics, one that gives special importance to political symbolism, life experiences, and feelings. That is what I have been arguing for in this book. But, the skeptical reader might ask, why bother going to such lengths? Why not simply speak of new governments and emergent social groups seeking legitimacy (as some of my critics think I should)? How can I justify having asked you to accompany me on this crooked path through kinship and ancestors, competition for believers, burial practices, property, authority, accountability, space, and time?

My reason is discomfort with the rationalistic and dry sense of politics that so many political analysts employ, particularly when dealing with postsocialist transformation. In my view, postsocialist politics is about much more than forming parties, having free elections, setting up independent banks, rewriting history books, or restoring property rights—complex though these be. To see dead-body politics in Eastern Europe as nothing more than revising the past toward legitimating new polities seems to me not wrong but impoverished. Rather, dead bodies have posthumous political life in the service of creating a newly meaningful universe. Their political work is to institute ideas about morality by assessing accountability and punishment, to sanctify space anew, to redefine the temporalities of daily life, to line people up with alternative ancestors and thereby to reconfigure the communities people participate in, and to attend to ancestors properly so they will fructify the enterprise of their descendants. By creating room in our analysis for ideas of this kind, we both look for things in postsocialist politics that we might otherwise ignore and also, I believe, enliven and enrich the study of politics in general, broadening and deepening what we understand it to mean.

Edwin Arlington Robinson wrote, "I will have more to say when I am dead." No matter which conceptions of cosmic order, ancestors, space, and time we human beings employ, it seems our dead, like Lenin, are always with us. The important thing is what we do with them.

NOTES

INTRODUCTION. CORPSES ON THE MOVE

1. This quotation also appeared in 1977 on a Soviet greeting card (see Tumarkin 1994: plate 20e). The card was sold for the 1977 anniversary of the Great October Revolution.

2. Information courtesy of Phyllis Mack, Rutgers University.

3. See Brown 1981; Geary 1978. For a present-day imagining of how such "translation" works, see Ellis Peters's novel *A Morbid Taste for Bones* (1987).

4. Information courtesy of Kirstie McClure, Johns Hopkins University.

5. Rumor had it that he had been fully submerged except for his nose, which had thus deteriorated, but this view is not universally accepted (see Morison 1959:407; *John Paul Jones* 1907). Thanks to Kathleen Much, Center for Advanced Study in the Behavioral Sciences, for this tidbit.

6. Tumarkin 1994:259.

7.   Dennie 1996. See, e.g., pp. 305ff. for some reburials.

8.   Cohen and Odhiambo 1992.

9.   See, for example, the dissertation research of anthropologists Carlota McAllister and Victoria Sanford.

10. See Brook Larmer, "Her Immortal Remains," *Newsweek* (16 December 1996), p. 67; and Richard O'Mara, "Eva Perón, Political Animal," *Baltimore Sun*, 1 January 1997, pp. E1–2. For more on Evita's remains, see Tomás Eloy Martínez's novel *Santa Evita* (1996).

11. Guber 1990.

12. *Newsweek* (27 April 1998), p. 39.

13. Initially the government gave permission only for him to be buried in his natal town, but Imelda continued to plan for a reburial in Manila: "We'll dig him up and move him down and bury him again. We do that all the time" (Christopher Brauchli, "The Chilling Adventures of Marcos' Corpse," *Baltimore Sun*, 28 May 1997, p. 9A.) My thanks to Reds Wolman for passing this article on to me.

14. Because none of the countries of the former Soviet bloc claimed to have reached the stage of "communism," calling themselves "socialist republics," I generally use the term "socialism," alternating on occasion with "communism" either for stylistic reasons or to signal specifically the Communist Party element of those regimes.

15. For Bulgaria, Maria Todorova (personal communication) states that there is far less political reburying than seems to be true elsewhere. An explanation might include the fact that the political transformation was less extreme there (this interpretation would fit Romania as well, where former communists also were a presence in post-1989 governments and where political reburials have not been numerous). For eastern Germany, see Christa Hasselhorst, "Kein Kult um berühmte Tote, nur stilles Gedenken an sie" (*Die Welt*, 13 November 1997, p. 27), which claims with some regret that Germany has no cult of its famous dead. Thanks to Paul Baltes for this reference.

     I should add that political reburial was a common practice in Eastern Europe even before the communist period. Romanians, for instance, reburied their first modern monarch, Alexandru Ioan Cuza—more than once. Cuza's embalmed body had been brought from Heidelberg, where he died in 1873, to his home in Ruginoasă; after seven years his bones were moved inside the church there. When the military front advanced too close in World War II, he was taken to the Trei Ierarhi Cathedral in Iași. There he was placed next to another peripatetic sovereign, Prince Dimitrie Cantemir, buried near Moscow at his death in 1723, exhumed in 1935, and brought to Iaşi for reburial (information courtesy of Sidonia Puiu, Biblioteca Academiei, Cluj, Romania). Hungarians also reburied many of their heroes, including several leaders of the 1848 revolution: Count Lajos Batthyány, Lajos Kossuth, and six executed generals (see Rév 1995; Lampland 1993). Even under the communists there were reburials, such as that of show-trial victim László Rajk in 1956. In 1939, Czechs dug up from the Sudeten area and reburied in Prague the remains of nineteenth-century poet Karel Hynek Mácha. And so on.

16. Thanks to Phyllis Mack for this observation.

17. Cf. Yampolsky 1995:107.

18. Information courtesy of David Harvey, Johns Hopkins University.

19. In Leningrad/St. Petersburg, several dozen now-unwanted statues are stored in the warehouse of the city's Museum of Culture (Victoria Voloshina, "Lenin to Be Buried Here," *Moscow News*, 3–9 April 1997, p. 3).

20. *The Times* (London), 26 November 1997, p. 17.

21. *Current Digest of the Soviet Press* 43 (30 October 1991):39.1.

22. I am much indebted to Gail Kligman, Claude Karnoouh, and Andrei Pop, who traveled to Budapest's Statue Park and made for me the slides reproduced here.

23. Information courtesy of Erika Woolf, University of Michigan.

24. The three statues of Antonescu erected by winter 1998 were at private expense. The first was raised in October 1993 near police headquarters in the city of Slobozia. According to rumor, it was planned and paid for in part by the Securitate-derived nationalist organization Vatra Românească.

25. Yampolsky 1995:104.

26. For example, Szelenyi and others argue for a distinctively socialist conception of urban space and function (see, e.g., Andrusz, Harloe, and Szelenyi 1996; French and Hamilton 1979). Campeanu (1994), Verdery (1996:chapter 2), and Yampolsky (1995) suggest peculiarities of socialist time.

27. Thanks to Dorothea von Mücke for a stimulating discussion on this point.

28. A *Moscow News* story on the blowing up of the new statues to Tsar Nicholas and Peter the Great shows how fuzzy is the line separating the two: "For centuries, people have been telling stories about statues coming to life, sometimes coming to haunt an offender, sometimes dragging one into the nether world. . . . [W]e look at them not as chunks of stone . . . but

as people, the city's good or evil geniuses" (Maria Chegodaeva, "Moscow Rates Its Monuments," *Moscow News*, 31 July–6 August 1997, p. 15). The same notion is found elsewhere, of course, such as in the play *Pygmalion* and the opera *Don Giovanni*.

29. Remnick 1996:45.

30. See the film *Eastern Europe: Breaking with the Past. #10: The Polish Experience* (Washington, D.C.: Global View Productions, 1990).

31. Yampolsky 1995:106.

32. These two examples were brought to my attention in a discussion with the Armenian ethnographer Levon Abrahamian.

33. See reports in *Current Digest of the Post-Soviet Press* 49 (1997): 13.22–23. The quote is directly from the fax sent by the group claiming responsibility.

34. Furthermore, they threatened that any "further harping on the blasphemous topic of 'reburying' the body of Vladimir Lenin will be met with fitting measures of proletarian revolutionary defense" (*Current Digest of the Post-Soviet Press* 49 [1997]: 27.13).

35. Moreover, Lenin continues to appear on occasion in Russian politics even now. Consider the following report from Armenian anthropologist Levon Abrahamian: "I spotted Lenin the last time on March 27th of 1997 in Moscow, at the nation-wide protest demonstration organized by the trade unions of Russia. A buffoon double of Lenin was protesting together with the poor against the government" (Abrahamian 1997:20).

36. Information courtesy of Irina Barnes, Stanford University.

37. Gal 1991. (The reburial occurred in 1988.) István Rév reports (personal communication) that the impetus for Bartók's removal was the approaching end of the fifty-year copyright on his compositions; his sons, wanting to increase their royalties before the copyright expired, hoped that by bringing him back, they would create demand for reeditions of his music.

38. Information courtesy of Daina Stukuls, University of Michigan.

39. Hauser 1995:81.

40. Information courtesy of Haldis Haukanes, University of Bergen.

41. *Internal* exiles were also important, as families sought to rebury their dead who had perished in communist prisons or labor camps. See the section "Anonymous Dead," below.

42. Information courtesy of István Rév.

43. Information courtesy of István Rév.

44. Information courtesy of Haldis Haukanes, University of Bergen.

45. Information courtesy of Daina Stukuls, University of Michigan.
46. Information courtesy of Michał Buchowski, University of Poznan. In Sikorski's case, there are doubts about whether it was really he who was flown back from England in the sealed coffin and interred under his name in Wawel Crypt (where only the most famous Poles are buried).
47. Thanks to Maria Todorova and Maria Heller for this information.
48. Information courtesy of Maria Todorova, University of Florida, Gainesville.
49. "Hungary Sadly Reflects on the Continuing Drain of Its Big Brains," *International Herald Tribune*, 21–22 March 1998, p. 5. Thanks to Jeremy King for this reference.
50. Rév 1995:36.
51. Ibid..21.
52. The juxtaposition of these two similar funerals suggested that the history intervening between Antall and Horthy had been excised (Rév 1995:32–33).
53. Dead bodies did not have to be buried and reburied to have political life. On 25 December 1989, for example, the corpses of the Ceauşescus were displayed on Romanian television in hopes of convincing Ceauşescu's supporters to stop fighting after he had fled.
54. Information courtesy of Andrew Lass, Mt. Holyoke College.
55. Trix 1997.
56. Judah 1997:39; Salecl 1996:421. Some of this information is from participants in a graduate seminar I held at the University of Chicago's Anthropology Department; I acknowledge their help gratefully, especially that of Marko Živković.
57. In early November 1997, the commission charged with deciding the tsar's fate postponed its decision for a second time, and the governor of Sverdlovsk Oblast (then housing him) objected that transit to Moscow might damage the bones or subject them to theft (*RFE/RL Newsline* 1 [52], part I [4 November 1997]). See also Alessandra Stanley, "Czar and Lenin Share Fate: Neither Can Rest in Peace," *New York Times*, 9 April 1997; A1, A4.
58. Arguments concerning the burials of Lenin and the tsar have another subtext: different political groups not only are trying to capture these bodies as powerful talismans but also are striving to set up competitive spiritual centers. Both those wanting to rebury the tsar in St. Petersburg and those wanting to bury Lenin there are engaged in a long-standing rivalry

between that city and Moscow for spiritual primacy in Russia (personal communication from Vyacheslav Karpov, Western Michigan University).

59. Information courtesy of Hermine DeSoto, University of Wisconsin.

60. It is likely, though I do not have the specifics, that bodies of Soviet soldiers in East European cemeteries are being moved from central to peripheral locations. Just such discussion occurred in Latvia, concerning the bodies of Soviet soldiers buried "too close" to the statue of Mother Latvia; the move discussed for them did not, however, take place. Information courtesy of Daina Stukuls, University of Michigan.

61. Paul Goble, "Russia: Analysis from Washington—Reburying the Past." *RFE/RL Newsline* no. 169 (17 June 1997).

62. Information courtesy of Maria Todorova, University of Florida. See also Creed 1995:849.

63. See, e.g., Hochschild 1994:199.

64. In Romania, a long-running television program called *Memorialul durerii* (The Memorial to Pain) has chronicled many such quests. Under the cryptocommunist Iliescu government (1990–1996), airing of the program was frequently obstructed. (I myself saw it only rarely during my research in 1993–1994 because it was given a very late-night slot and was often moved unannounced even from that.)

65. A Mass was then held in memory of the victims. See Tumarkin 1994: 176–181.

66. From the other side, Nina Tumarkin details ongoing efforts to give proper burial to the Soviet soldiers killed in World War II; in 1991 alone, one such organization found and buried 18,349 unidentified soldiers (some of them doubtless Nazis) (Tumarkin 1994:15). This initiative is not new but has been going on since the war ended.

67. See, for example, the catalog in Pippidi 1995.

68. Taussig 1997:100.

69. Feeley-Harnik 1991:xxi.

70. Koselleck 1994:10. My thanks to Margret Baltes for her help with this work.

I. DEAD BODIES ANIMATE THE STUDY OF POLITICS

1. My thanks to Fay Cook and Laura Stoker for two stimulating conversations about "politics."

2. See, e.g., Harvey 1989.

3. See Verdery 1996:chapter 1. I will not take up here the many questions my

phrasing points to—such as whether there is such a thing as "capitalism," whether "socialist" systems were a form of state capitalism or something sui generis, etc.

4. Nor do I mean the concept of "framing," with which some political scientists think to bring in culture by showing how politicians package something so it sells (e.g., Snow et al. 1986; Snow and Benford 1992). I borrow my phrasing from Doug McAdam, whom I thank for his assistance with this paragraph.

5. I am indebted to conversations with Fay Cook, Lynn Hunt, and Kirstie McClure that helped me to see this as my goal.

6. For a similar critique, see Karl 1990. My thanks to her, as well, for a helpful conversation on the themes of democratization and legitimacy.

7. Comaroff and Comaroff 1998.

8. See Platz 1997; Verdery 1996: chapter 7; and Ries 1997.

9. E.g., Urban 1997.

10. Jowitt 1987.

11. See, e.g., Butler 1990, 1993; Bynum 1995a, 1995b; Scarry 1985.

12. My thanks to István Rév, Laura Stoker, and Dorothea von Mücke for stimulating my thoughts on this question.

    Jean and John Comaroff (personal communication) offer a different answer to the "Why dead bodies?" question from the one I present here. They suggest that changes in the global economy have made the body (as raw labor power) the only salable commodity that everyone has, and that advances in the process of its commodification (the sale of organs and sexual services, the marketing of smiles, etc.) place it at the forefront of capitalist development.

13. István Rév employs this argument in his discussion of the "Why dead bodies" question (the work is in progress under the title *Covering History*). I am grateful to him for sharing it with me.

14. Brown 1981:86.

15. This is not to say that such "construals" are unconstrained. Efforts to grapple with the problem of what impedes the complete invention of pasts include those of Michel-Rolph Trouillot in his book *Silencing the Past* (1995) and (quite differently) of Milan Kundera, in *The Book of Laughter and Forgetting* (1980). Both see checks on invention as coming from the *materiality* of certain objects and processes. The hat of Clementis on Gottwald's head in the opening scene of Kundera's novel, the packets of letters, the flash of a gold tooth   all signal events and people who cannot

be simply airbrushed out of history. Although we can variously interpret the *meanings* of these material things, we cannot make them up—or unmake them—entirely. I am grateful to Michel-Rolph Trouillot for a stimulating conversation on this theme.

16. Most symbols share these properties. I claim only that corpses are particularly effective in politics because they embody the properties unusually well.

17. My account draws on those of Gal 1989, 1998; Rév 1995; and Bruszt and Stark 1992.

18. Barber (1988:49) observes, however, that people may bury a corpse facedown when they fear it is dangerous; this posture will make the corpse burrow further into the earth rather than emerge from his grave.

19. The initiative for Nagy's reburial did not come from official circles, but from the Hungarian diaspora (who had organized an anniversary in Paris the year before) and from the families of Nagy and others hanged with him or purged later. The families had repeatedly sought official permission but were put off. At length the Hungarian government agreed to a small family burial, then (under pressure) to a nonofficial public funeral; from that point on, the government had nothing to do with the arrangements. By the time of the funeral, however, the Party leadership was so divided and its position in society so compromised that they asked to be included! The initiating families at first refused, then finally agreed that three officials could attend as private persons; they would be excluded from the private family burial that followed the public gathering. For those who would see Nagy's reburial as a political effort to build legitimacy for the communist regime, I note that it should, rather, be seen as crucial to the Party's downfall (see Rév 1995:24; Bruszt and Stark 1992:40).

20. Gal 1989:8–9.

21. For a book-length study of comparable funeral politics in South Africa, see Garrey Dennie's fascinating dissertation (Dennie 1996).

22. These cosmic associations contribute to the well-known ethnological fact that death rituals are the slowest of all practices to change (Barber 1988:48; Brown 1981:24; Kligman 1988). Their stability, in turn, makes them good instruments for nationalists who—as sometimes happens with new regimes—want to reaffirm a connection with or return to "older" national "traditions." Claims of that kind have been rampant in building anticommunist identities since 1989. (Thanks to Pam Ballinger for suggesting this point.)

23. For a particularly interesting treatment, see Obeyesekere 1990.

24. Anderson 1983:4, 141.
25. For a fascinating discussion of this point, see Williams, in progress.
26. One might inspect for their capital-forming effects the different kinds of dead bodies into which I grouped my examples in the introduction. "Local Boys Made Good" return home before an international audience that probably didn't even know Bartók was Hungarian or Ionesco Romanian, though it was certainly familiar with those men. They are repatriated as cultural treasures, proof that this or that country is part of European civilization and thus, e.g., worthy of NATO membership. Corpses whose fame is more localized enter into *internal* political competitions in which each participant hopes to compete more favorably by "funding" his campaign with the political or cultural capital of specific allies who are dead. And the anonymous dead provide the same for would-be politicians looking to speak on behalf of "our [victimized] people," a use for which it is precisely their nameless-ness that counts.
27. I am indebted to Gail Kligman for the help she provided me in thinking about the issues contained in this section, both in conversation and in her *Wedding of the Dead* (1988).
28. See, e.g., Bourdieu 1977:164–171.
29. Before pooh-poohing the idea that "regular" people leading "regular" lives worry much about this sort of thing, note that some 70 percent of the U.S. population believes in angels—a fact that throws light on why the TV program *Touched by an Angel* has such high ratings.

    Perhaps I might illustrate the "cosmic" in the "everyday" for Eastern Europe with one of its most widespread and popular folktales. The tale appears all across Southeastern Europe but is particularly well crystallized in Romania. It has caught the imagination of folk both learned and not, and my own experience indicates that it still does. The story in outline concerns a young shepherd who sees his favorite lamb sorrowing, and asks her why. She tells him that she has overheard his two companions scheming to kill him. Knowing that animals can foresee the future, he believes her, then proceeds to tell her how he wants his funeral to be handled; his wishes show popular beliefs that violent deaths of the young require special treatment and, in the case of an unmarried person, a symbolic wedding so that his life can have included all the major components of human existence. He wants to be buried not in a church cemetery but in the meadow, with his sheep singing the funeral laments, and pines and stars as wedding/funeral guests.

According to Eliade, the tale's most profound message is the shepherd's will to change the meaning of his destiny, turning it into a moment in a cosmic liturgy. By taking the folk practice of the "death-wedding" and making it a cosmic event, he succeeds in transforming a dire event into a sacrament, thus triumphing over his own fate. Folk balladeers as well as intellectuals who love the tale find in it an affinity between the shepherd's destiny and that of the Romanian people. The shepherd has made an absurd event meaningful by responding to adversity with a new spiritual creation (Eliade 1970:251–254). For more on the Romanian form of this tale, see Kligman 1988; Stahl 1983.

30. Anthropologists have expanded their notion of culture beyond the ideational, but other usage for the most part has not. I thus find it preferable not to use the word at all, in hopes that my meaning will be better grasped.

   Victoria Bonnell (1997) speaks of "cultural repertoires" to get at some of the problems I am addressing. Like me, she wants to emphasize the variety of symbols and meanings that can be brought into play in social action. She differs in drawing her notion of culture from Clifford Geertz, whereas I draw mine from Pierre Bourdieu.

31. I use the plural to indicate the plurality of solutions to the problem, for which no single cosmology is adequate either across the region or within its several countries.

32. Thanks to Michael Burawoy for a very stimulating exchange on this theme.

33. See Joas 1993.

34. For further discussion of this point, see Verdery 1996:chapter 3, and references there.

35. A refreshing exception is Jowitt 1987.

36. I say "renewal" rather than something else (revival, resuscitation) because although religious worship was highly constrained in socialist systems, it was also *institutionalized* (albeit in a lesser role than before), not banned altogether. Ministries of "Cults," lists of accepted and prohibited faiths, in some cases state salaries for priests—all these kept religion present in certain forms throughout the communist period. What is taking place now is mostly not a revival of something banned but a renewal, expansion, and reinstitutionalization of something already there. In the cases of churches that were prohibited, however, such as the Greek Catholic Church and the Jehovah's Witnesses, we are of course dealing with full-scale revivals.

37. Durkheim 1915; Elias 1992; and Leach 1961. One might argue that there is

also an irreducible *reality* to space and time (there is measurable surface between two points, and there is a measurable gap between two moments). I am more interested here, however, in how notions and experiences of time and space can be modified through social activity.

38. For three examples, see Hareven's (1982) arguments about "family time" and "industrial time"; Nancy Munn's (1986) gendered spatiotemporalities of renown; and Ann Lovell's (1992) research on the "time" of homeless people in the United States.

39. See Verdery 1996:chapter 2.

40. According to Walter Benjamin, when fighting erupted, "the clocks in towers were fired upon simultaneously and independently from several places in Paris. An eyewitness wrote as follows: 'Who would have believed it! We are told that new Joshuas at the foot of every tower, as though irritated with time itself, fired at the dials in order to stop the day' " (Benjamin 1969:262).

41. See, for instance, Binns 1979–1980; Thompson 1967; Verdery 1996:chapter 2; Zerubavel 1981.

42. I do not regard this concept as having cross-cultural or cross-temporal validity, but for purposes of this discussion I will act as if it does.

43. E.g., Slezkine 1994; Verdery 1996:chapter 4; and Vujačić and Zaslavsky 1991.

44. See, e.g., Connell 1987, 1990.

45. An especially interesting discussion of the link between nationalism and kinship is found in Delaney 1994; see also Schneider 1977.

46. Anderson 1983:5.

47. It is not only the relations of living and dead that are at stake in a proper burial: additionally, in many societies it takes a proper burial for the deceased to become fully a "person," embedded in a specific set of social relations (a specific community of mourners) and ready for incorporation into a specific set of already dead souls (ancestors, in fully kin-based societies, and ancestors plus others, elsewhere). Proper burial creates these communities, drawing boundaries that include some possible mourners and exclude others, invoking connections with some and not other already dead souls. See the discussion in Rév 1995:25–26, 30.

48. Feeley-Harnik 1991a:47, 51. See also Barraud et al. 1994; Bloch and Parry 1982; Huntington and Metcalf 1979; Turner 1957:295.

49. These are abundantly illustrated in Paul Barber's *Vampires, Burial, and Death* (1988); I bring in others as well, from former Yugoslavia, Romania,

Hungary, and Ukraine. See, e.g., Eliade 1955, 1970; Halpern and Halpern 1972; Kligman 1988; McNally and Florescu 1972; and Young 1997. I am grateful to Andrey Arkhipov, Stanford University, for information on Ukraine.

50. Personal communication from the three scholars.

51. In places that take ancestors seriously, it is virtually universal that the relations of living and dead are maintained through commensality, just as is true among live people (cf. Kligman 1988:157–159, 192–194).

52. Barber suggests the more sinister possibility that giving the dead food and drink will keep them full, so they have less need of human flesh and blood (1988:48). Interestingly, in some parts of Romania the word for the cemetery plot is the same as the word for one's landholding: *moşia* (information courtesy of Dr. Ion Cuceu, Institute of Ethnography, Cluj, Romania). One might remember this in connection with my argument about ancestors, nations, and soil in chapter 3.

53. This custom is very old. Caroline Bynum describes it for Roman burials in the second and third centuries (Bynum 1995a:53–55). Peter Brown reports that in the fourth century, priests strove to stop congregations from feasting at the graves of the dead, seeing this practice as a resurgence of paganism; it was eventually incorporated into Christianity, however (Brown 1981:26, 29).

   Aside from these annual practices there is the regular commemoration of the dead in periodic church services. In Romanian the service is called *parastas*, and it consists of the priest's mentioning the names of the departed at specific intervals—three days after the death, nine days, forty days, six months, a year, and so on. For those attending the service, the next of kin provide food (*pomană*) in the form of plum brandy and a special kind of bread.

54. I am grateful to Andrey Arkhipov (Stanford University) for sharing with me the results of his research in the Poland/Ukraine border region. Other details come from Andreesco and Bacou 1986. (Thanks to Sandra Pralong for bringing this book to my attention.)

55. Tumarkin 1994:125–126.

56. The site usually mentioned is with his family in Leningrad/St. Petersburg.

57. *Current Digest of the Soviet Press* 43 (1991):45.23. I saw Peter Jennings retract the ABC news story, though I did not see the original report.

58. Perhaps he thought that to bury Lenin would convince Western skeptics that Russia's democratization was sure. When he brought up the idea in 1997, he

proposed to "rid Red Square of its status as a cemetery" by referendum ("We Will Bury You: Russian President Boris Yeltsin Proposes Referendum on Giving Vladimir Lenin's Corpse a Christian Burial," *Maclean's* 110, no. 24 [16 June 1997]: 35).

59. *Moscow News* (English ed.) no. 29 (10–16 June 1997): 2. Burial was opposed more by older people than by younger, and by the less rather than the more educated. People with religious faith were in favor of burial more than were nonbelievers.

60. In writing of the endless line to get into the mausoleum during the 1960s, Todorov observes that if each person has 80 seconds, and if no one else is ever born, it will take 10,147 years for the whole human race to bid farewell to Lenin (1995:147). The mummy, he proposes, signifies "the primal symbolic point of the entire space which opens above and around it .... It is the capital that props up the structure of the Brave New World" (pp. 126–127). "Lenin['s] body became the primal Party nucleus of power .... Stalin's speech began with the following words: 'We, the communists, are people of a special make. We are made of a special material.' The communist body does not decay! The Mummy is the greatest communist" (p. 143).

61. Robin Lodge, "Lenin's Embalmers Reveal the Secrets of Their Art," *The Times* (London), 26 November 1997, p. 17.

62. These points are discussed in Tumarkin 1983:chapter 1 and p. 200; Berdiaev 1937:chapter 1.

63. I should note the wording of the poll whose finding was that he should be buried: "In accordance with your ideas about the Russian Orthodox tradition of burying the dead, what, in your opinion, would be the right thing to do with the body of Vladimir Ilyich Lenin?" *Moscow News* (English ed.) no. 29 (10–16 July 1997): 2; see also *Current Digest of the Post-Soviet Press* 49 (1997):24.14. Because the question predisposed a response in religious terms, the sorts of beliefs I have been discussing are very relevant to the poll's results.

64. Some of the bad things that can happen are presented in Barber 1988. In addition, I am very grateful to Andrey Arkhipov for explaining to me some of the ideas about proper burial that feed into the debates about Lenin.

65. See Robert Hertz's famous work on death (Hertz 1960), in which he shows that, ethnographically speaking, exhumation and reburial may in fact be the norm, not a departure.

66. Danforth and Tsiaras 1982.

67. Again, this idea is not limited to Eastern Europe. Recall the hero of Gabriel García Márquez's novella *Of Love and Other Demons,* who carries his dead daughter around in a suitcase, trying to prove her worthy of sanctification because she remains young and beautiful, and because her hair continues to grow.

68. See also Bonnell 1997:149.

69. Information courtesy of Vyacheslav Karpov, Western Michigan University.

70. As if the debate on Lenin's burial were not complex enough, there have been reports that scientists have plans to *clone* him. The attitudes Russian citizens expressed to an interviewer for National Public Radio in May 1997 ranged from indifferent to vengeful. One person said, "Cloning Lenin makes no sense—he's a figure of the past. We should be cloning a genius, like Einstein," whereas another thought that Lenin should be cloned so people could punish him for all the wrongs he had committed (National Public Radio, *Morning Edition,* 15 May 1997).

71. Kligman 1988; see also Andreesco and Bacou 1986. Barber notes (1988:78) the great antiquity of these forms of disposing of the dead.

72. Information courtesy of Andrey Arkhipov, Stanford University. A different way of stating the matter is a comment by Ilya Zbarsky, whose father was involved in the first embalming of Lenin in 1924: "It is not a tradition of Russian people, of civilized people in general, to make relics of heads of state" (information courtesy of Caroline Humphrey, Cambridge University).

73. Andreesco and Bacou 1986:19–20, 60–61, 63, 118–119, 179–180, 216, 232.

74. Hobsbawm and Ranger 1983.

75. Andreesco and Bacou 1986.

76. Thanks to Gerald Creed for this information. See Chuck Sudetic, "For Well-housed Dead, TV and Other Comforts," *New York Times,* 19 February 1991, p. A4.

77. See Verdery 1996:chapter 6.

78. One might fruitfully pursue this method for many other concepts involved in the postsocialist transformation—such as, for instance, power. Cambridge University anthropologist Caroline Humphrey explores the contrast between "Western" notions of power and those of Russians, as contained in the words *khozyaistvo* (domain, from *khozyain,* master) and *vlast'* (power). According to Humphrey, Russians see power and sociopolitical order as

> brought about by the exercise of centralised and personified power, not by law, [etc.]. . . . Crucially, this idea is also represented in the

term for the state (*gosudarstvo*), deriving from *gosudar'* (the sovereign). I am arguing here that the cultural concepts of the 'domain' (*khozyaistvo*) and the state (*gosudarstvo*) encode in themselves from the very beginning the reification of political entities in which a central personification of power creates order. . . . The nightmare of chaos, in this way of thinking, is counteracted by the exercise of power . . . [based in] the personality of the master (*khozyain*), who is honed and dedicated to power such that he becomes one of the naturally existing powers (*vlasti*). (Humphrey 1996/7:77–78)

Such a view of power has clear implications for political change in Russia.

79. Dan Balz, "19th-Century Chief Is Returning Home from London Grave," *San Jose Mercury News*, 26 September 1997, p. 22A.

80. In February 1998 a controversy arose over the return of the Winnie-the-Pooh dolls from New York to England. The instigator of this move argued that the toys looked "very unhappy indeed," adding, "I'm not surprised, considering they have been incarcerated in a foreign country for all these years." She went on to compare the toys to the Parthenon Marbles in the British Museum, saying Britons wanted the dolls every bit as much as the Greeks wanted the marbles (Dan Barry, "Back Home to Pooh Corner? Forget It, New York Says," *New York Times*, 5 February 1998, pp. A1, A20). My thanks to Phyllis Mack for drawing this controversy to my attention.

81. Greenfield 1989.

82. The German notion of *Blut und Boden* expresses the connection nicely.

83. For one thing, he died recently enough to have relatives alive who wanted his body back—something that would be less true of, say, Ferencz Rákóczi, who died in Turkey in 1735. For another, Hungary seems to be unusual in its political tradition of reburying. Rév attributes this to peculiarities of Hungarian history: "Hungarian history is a history of battles lost, and consequently a continuous history of executions, exiles, and political suicides. The normal public rituals of Hungarian history are, accordingly, not victory parades but funerals and reburials" (1995: 31). Other things may contribute as well—such as religious differences, with the Roman Catholic and Eastern Orthodox churches more prone than Protestant ones to traffic in relics and other fascinations with the dead. Perhaps cases also differ in the role of ancestor worship in popular devotions.

84. This kind of explanation has been offered for phenomena comparable with the ones I discuss. In Nina Tumarkin's discussion of the Lenin cult, for example, she states that its "evident purpose . . . was to strengthen the perceived legitimacy of the party's authority." Similarly with Khrushchev's resuscitation of the cult during the 1960s: "[i]n its totality the Lenin cult was designed and maintained to . . . provide [the Communist Party] with legitimacy that was unassailable" (Tumarkin 1983:98, 260).

2. THE RESTLESS BONES OF BISHOP INOCHENTIE MICU

1. The name is pronounced In-o-kent-yeh Mee-koo (with accent on the penultimate syllable of both). Following the example of historian David Prodan, I use this form of the name. He was born Ioan Micu, later adopting Inochentie as his monastic name and sometimes hyphenating or simply appending the surname Klein, which is the rendering of Micu in German. His full designation is Ioan Inochentie Micu-Klein, Baron de Sad. Although some people refer to him as Inocenţiu, Prodan asserts (personal communication) that both Inochentie and his historian nephew Samuil Micu-Klein used the spelling I (therefore) employ.

2. I conducted some field research on Inochentie while in Romania during June and July 1997, for work on a different topic (decollectivization), financed by a National Science Foundation grant. I emphasize that my results are correspondingly impressionistic rather than conclusive. In particular, I was unable to secure interviews with anyone in the hierarchy of the Romanian Orthodox Church in Bucharest, despite considerable effort. My discussions with Orthodox clerics were limited to one village priest in Transylvania, the head monk of a Bucharest monastery, and a well-known Bucharest parish priest. I supplemented these with articles from a publication called *Scara*, which is not an official publication of the church but includes writings from some of its top officials. On the Greek Catholic side, I spoke in Bucharest with a priest and with a former member of Iliescu's cabinet, and in Transylvania with the rector of a Greek Catholic theological seminary, an elderly priest and a university professor who both had been active in the return of Inochentie's bones, the Greek Catholic priest-cum-senator who had been pressing for legislative resolution of the matter of church buildings, and a number of Greek Catholic (as well as Orthodox) parish members. In addition, the magazine *Vatra* conducted a survey in which readers were asked to write in with their views on the contribution of

the Greek Catholic Church to Romanian history; I had access to twenty-six of these responses. Regular perusal of the wider Romanian press contributed further information.

3. In the terms to be introduced below, the priest who wanted publicity is Greek Catholic; the others, Orthodox.

4. In the summer of 1994 I happened to share a plane from Bucharest with a group of Baptists who had spent the preceding months in Russia and Romania. Those with whom I spoke had worked mostly with "captives"—people in prisons and orphanages—and had held high-level talks with the Ministries of Education toward introducing religious teaching into Russian and Romanian textbooks. They seemed to regard the two countries as a virgin field for evangelizing, as if official atheism during the communist period had wiped out all vestiges of religious belief.

5. For assistance with this chapter I am grateful to Sister Carol E. Wheeler of the Baltimore Sisters of Mercy and most particularly to the Reverend Mr. Ronald Roberson of the Secretariat for Ecumenical and Interreligious Affairs, National Conference of Catholic Bishops, Washington, D.C., who read a draft and offered detailed corrections.

6. The eyes through which we see it are those of a Greek Catholic priest I met in the Transylvanian city of Cluj, who claimed to have visited the actual site.

7. Albu 1983:224–225. Mrs. Victoria Lascu of Cluj informs me that these words were taken from Ovid's letters written during his exile from Rome in what is today Romania. The passage quoted here is followed, in Ovid, by another in which he states that a Scythian exiled in Rome would miss his homeland every bit as much as a Roman exiled in Scythia.

8. Transylvania signed the 1648 Peace of Westphalia as a sovereign entity.

9. See Prodan 1971.

10. These were the use of unleavened bread, the addition of Purgatory to Heaven and Hell as postmortem destinations, and the "filioque" (the acknowledgment in the Creed that the Holy Spirit of the Trinity proceeds from both the Father *and* the Son). The combination church that resulted from this union could thus be widely adopted with minimal disruption, for very few village priests comprehended the finer points of doctrine (usually written in Latin, which hardly any Romanian clerics could understand), and to their followers the changes were virtually unobservable—and often unobserved.

11. By the early eighteenth century, either Habsburg action or other efforts of the Counter-Reformation had set up Greek Catholic churches in parts of

what are now western Ukraine, eastern Poland, northeast Hungary, eastern Slovakia, and Transylvania.

12. The count, carried out by Inochentie Micu shortly after taking office as
bishop, yielded 2,742 Greek Catholics in over 85,000 families, and only 458
Orthodox priests (Albu 1983:119).

13. There were two different versions of this promise. The first, which appears
in the Leopoldine Diploma of 1699, following upon the Act of Union of
1698, states clearly that Uniate *clergy* will be freed of feudal obligations; the
second, in the Leopoldine Diploma of 1701 (which was somehow "lost"
from the early 1700s until "recent times" [Prodan 1971:127]), made this
same promise to *all* Romanians who would join the union.

14. Although the year of his birth has been customarily given as 1692, his biog-
rapher Francisc Pall has recalculated it as 1700 (Pall 1997).

15. In addition to his evident motive of raising his people up, the claims he
defended would have the effect of consolidating the new Greek Catholic
institution by assuring it of revenues and equal political status. It is in any
case clear that money was always on Micu's mind. Whenever the Habsburg
court would send word that they expected his church to contribute something—such as for the army Empress Maria Theresa needed in order to
secure her throne, or for some construction project—he would reply that
until the conditions of the union were met, he had no funds for such contributions (see, e.g., Albu 1983:112, 132).

16. See Prodan's (1971) outstanding work so titled.

17. Ibid.:187. Inochentie's contribution was of several kinds. First, as mentioned above, he had the genius to take a language deriving from the feudal system of social categories and turn it into an ethnonational claim. He
began the systematic argument for Romanians' antiquity in Transylvania
as the "sons of Rome," thus making political an unelaborated piece of historical miscellany. By founding schools and arranging for scholarships
through which Greek Catholics could obtain an education, he laid the basis
for an educated elite that would later develop the national movement he
initiated; that is, he used education as a substitute for the routes to privilege
(landed wealth, political office, manufacturing) that the other nations in
Transylvania monopolized.

18. As Simion Bărnuțiu (himself a product of Greek Catholic schooling) put
it in 1848, "Oh unhappy children! Who will defend you if your parents join
hands with foreigners against you? . . . Together with the Union came
hatred between Romanians. . . . Wouldn't the Hungarians have been much

more impressed by a united people . . . than by one scattered across disparate parties?" (Albu 1983:68, 70).

19. In 1744 an Orthodox revival broke out in southern Transylvania. Its cause was the visit of an Orthodox monk (Visarion Sarai) sent by the Orthodox archbishop of Serbia for this very purpose. Visarion's work was abetted by Protestant nobles disturbed at the Habsburgs' success with catholicization and at increased flight of the Orthodox serfs who refused it. When Inochentie responded to the Orthodox revival by suggesting that Romanians were abjuring the union and fleeing because they had never received the benefits promised them (indeed, throughout the decade Greek Catholic clergy were found to be saying precisely that), the Diet passed this on to Empress Maria Theresa as evidence of his potential apostasy (Prodan 1971:162–164). Precisely *what* Inochentie said remains unclear. In one of the standard works on the history of Orthodox–Greek Catholic relations, Romanian (Orthodox) historian Silviu Dragomir quotes from two Austrian sources the following exchange in the 1737 Transylvanian Diet, where Inochentie was once again protesting nonimplementation of the promises tied to the union. If we do not obtain these rights, he said, "Clerum meum in dubio hererit" (my clergy will remain in doubt). A Hungarian baron exclaimed, according to Dragomir, that this meant Greek Catholics were not really Catholic in belief, merely pursuing material advantages; to which Inochentie reportedly replied that to get their rights, they would even "turn Turk" (Dragomir 1920:134). The Greek Catholic priest who showed me these passages expressed his own doubts about the validity of both Dragomir's interpretation (which in turn borrows from the earlier work of Augustin Bunea) and his translation of the original Austrian sources; this particular translation is what sustains the Orthodox claim that Inochentie and other Greek Catholics planned to abjure the union and return to the Orthodox fold.

20. I heard at least three separate claims as to who had initiated Inochentie's return. One attributed it to Bucharest-based government Greek Catholics; another, to a Cluj-based group of Greek Catholic clerics and laypersons; and a third, to the Vatican's papal nuncio in Romania. Clearly all three could have acted in concert, and with others; I cannot say who proposed the idea first. One name figures among those who helped pay the costs of Inochentie's return: Iosif Constantin Drăgan, a controversial Milan-based Romanian émigré with dubious past ties to the interwar fascists as well as to the Ceauşescu regime (see *Unirea* 8, no. 8 [August 1997]: 2).

A small body of potential folklore developed around the reburial. One item was that a "lobby" of Greek Catholics from Romania (in opposition to those from Ukraine) pressured the pope to receive President Iliescu's delegation so it could petition for return of the bones. Initially uninterested in this idea, the pope was reportedly persuaded to support it because of active Orthodox resistance to giving back church properties to Romania's Greek Catholics. A second tidbit concerns exactly *whose* bones were returned to Transylvania in August 1997. One of the obstacles to bringing Inochentie home to Transylvania was that flooding in the monastery where he was buried had disturbed the graves of others buried there. According to two Greek Catholic priests with whom I spoke, Inochentie's bones had remained intact in his heavy sarcophagus, but other bones had been collected and thrown into it along with his. I have no idea how the bones were sorted so as to send to Transylvania only the ones belonging to Inochentie.

21. Plans for his return were afoot for many decades. There was one in the period between the two world wars—"somehow it just never got off the ground," said the amiable priest who told me of it. Another plan surfaced in the 1970s, supposedly initiated not by Greek Catholics—they were illegal then—but by Ceauşescu. He proposed it as a way of creating an easily supervised Bucharest-centered metachurch from Romania's Roman and Greek Catholic and Orthodox churches. Bringing home the most famous person whose life united all three would facilitate that. This plan reportedly foundered on the machinations of Greek Catholics in the Vatican, who refused to turn their hero's body over to be reburied by the odious Romanian Orthodox hierarchy, staunch collaborators with the godless Communist Party. (I have this report from a Greek Catholic monk.)

22. The only country in which the Greek Catholic Church was not forced to merge with the Orthodox Church was Hungary.

23. See, e.g., Cipăianu 1997; Turcuş 1997. That Greek Catholics also represented Romanian national identity made them even more anathema to a party aiming to dissolve nationalisms into internationalism.

24. Technically speaking, the confiscated church properties belong to the Romanian state, not the Orthodox Church, to which the state merely assigned rights of use. During the 1990s the conflict proceeded, however, as if the Orthodox Church were the proprietor. Only a decision of the government's Legislative Council in October 1997, declaring the state as proprietor, suggested something other than that the Orthodox Church would

be the one to resolve the question (see *Adevărul*, 18–19 October 1997, p. 4).

25. Pusztai (1997) reports similar outdoors services among Greek Catholics in Ukraine.

26. According to one Greek Catholic priest, Romanian Patriarch Teoctist actually gave an order to Orthodox priests in Transylvania to prevent Greek Catholicism, *by any means*, from reestablishing itself. The motive suggested was that he saw Greek Catholic clergy as responsible for efforts to have him removed from his post after 1989.

27. According to the 1992 census, Greek Catholics numbered 228,337 (compared with 1.5 million in 1948), or 1 percent of Romania's population; Orthodox numbered 19,762,135 (86.8 percent). (*Recensămîntul populaţiei şi al locuinţelor din 7 ianuarie 1992* [Bucharest, 1992], p. xiii). Greek Catholics dispute this figure, however, claiming that they were underenumerated and that many persons had said they would not declare themselves Greek Catholic until the property question was clarified so they could worship in peace. The papal nuncio has estimated the number at around four hundred thousand, which is doubtless high (information courtesy of Rev. Mr. Ronald Roberson).

28. The 1992 census gives the distribution of Romania's population as 54 percent urban and 46 percent rural, with 63 percent of Uniates living in urban and 37 percent in rural locations (ibid.).

29. Lelia Munteanu, "Biserica Ardealului trezeşte ţara," *Adevărul*, 24 March 1998, (http://adevarul.kappa.ro).

30. The bill proposed that wherever Greek Catholics have re-formed a congregation and there is more than one church building, they should receive one. Where there is only one building, it will be used alternately by both faiths until a second building can be constructed.

Given their relatively small numbers, it may seem surprising that the Greek Catholics have the political strength to get such a bill as far as it went (much less to persuade former apparatchik President Iliescu to petition Rome for the return of Inochentie's bones!). They are disproportionately represented in the National Peasant Christian Democratic Party, the single most powerful group in the post-1996 reform government; and at least two very influential ministers in Iliescu's cabinet were Greek Catholics.

31. The paper *22* published a number of statements by Orthodox archbishops, some declaring they would not obey the law if it were passed, others warning of catastrophic ethnic conflict in Transylvania if it were. See Gabriel Andreescu, "Principală ameninţare la adresa democraţiei: Ierarhia Bisericii

Ortodoxe Române." *22* (24–30 June 1997): 9. See also Anca Manolescu, "O lecție pentru societatea civilă," *Dilema* 5 (4–10 July 1997): 11.

32. See Floca 1993. The idea that the church building belongs to the believers may be more prevalent (and of greater longevity) in village communities, where people see the building as the product of their common labor in raising it up (Prof. Mihai Pop, personal communication).

33. This was the view of the Greek Catholics with whom I spoke, mainly Cluj intellectuals, but is also reported by Kligman (personal communication) as the common view of parishioners of all types in Maramureș, northern Transylvania.

34. Figures from *Adevărul*, 22 September 1977; pp. 1, 3a. At the time of a newspaper report on this project, the prevailing exchange rate would make the cost of the trillion-lei cathedral about $145 billion—an astronomical sum, given the church's (and Romania's) financial resources.

35. Information courtesy of Gail Lapidus. See also the excellent work of Hungarian ethnographer Bertalan Pusztai (1997) on the conflicts involving Hungarian Greek Catholics in Ukraine, whose situation differs greatly from that of Romania's Greek Catholics in that it is not Orthodox but Roman Catholics who deny Greek Catholics their church buildings.

36. The most celebrated such case is that of Archbishop Nicolae Corneanu of the Banat, who, while holding a service to turn over to Greek Catholics a church building in Lugoj, offered them a public apology for his collaboration. See also Gabriel Andreescu, "Declarațiile IPS Corneanu și colaborationismul Bisericii Ortodoxe Române," *22* (18–24 March 1997): 6.

37. This figure was given me by an Orthodox monk who seemed credible in other respects, so I accept it provisionally.

38. Internal strife of a comparable sort has also emerged within other Orthodox churches, such as the Bulgarian, Estonian, and Ukrainian, resulting in open splits. Each has at least two factions, an "anticommunist" one and a "traditionalist" one that is sometimes also pro-Moscow. In some countries of the former Soviet Union, the problem reflects divisions among Russians resident there, who are Orthodox (the majority population—Estonians, Latvians, etc.—being Catholic or Protestant) but who are divided between allegiance to the Russian Orthodox Church and the Orthodox churches established in these countries (such as the Estonian Apostolic Orthodox Church, loyal to the patriarch of Constantinople). The Ukrainian case is the most complex, for the Orthodox Church there has split into at least *three* fragments: the Ukrainian Orthodox Church–Moscow Patriarchate, the

Ukrainian Orthodox Church–Kiev Patriarchate, and the Ukrainian Autocephalous Orthodox Church (itself split into two factions). These fight among themselves over doctrine, property, and matters of organization. (See *RFE/RL Newsline*, no. 190, part II [7 January 1998].) To complicate things further, Greek Catholics are also numerous in western Ukraine (over a million live there), and they have talked of making the Greek Catholic Church a "national church."

39. Archbishop Nicolae Corneanu of the Banat, sometimes mentioned as an alternative, has drawn considerable notice to himself by siding with Greek Catholics on the property question and by other moves indicating an open-mindedness not heretofore in evidence at the top of the hierarchy. Archbishop Bartolomeu Anania of Cluj, by contrast, has been occupying the niche of archconservative, launching diatribes against homosexuality and other topics of interest to the pro-Western reformists. He was one of the two archbishops to announce publicly his refusal to comply with the law on giving back churches to the Greek Catholics, as soon as this law passed the lower house of Parliament.

40. St. Paraschiva herself returned from Greece a few centuries ago, bought by the *voivod* Vasile Lupu to be housed in the famous Cathedral of the Three Bishops (Trei Ierarhi) he had built in Iaşi. It is said that Lupu paid a lot of money for St. Paraschiva's remains, since the Turks opposed transporting dead bodies across borders.

41. See, e.g., Oţetea 1970:275. The communists suppressed this view only briefly (ca. 1950–1965).

42. See Roberson 1995:207, which cites a text by Archbishop of Transylvania Antonie Plămădeală.

43. See, e.g., the following pages in the *Vatra* readers' survey on the role of the Greek Catholic Church in Romanian history: *Vatra* (1996): no. 11–12, pp. 57–59 and (1997): no. 1, pp. 66–69. One instance of the Greek Catholic position is the following lead sentence from an article in a Greek Catholic newspaper: "The Romanian people are ethnically the son of imperial Rome, and religiously the son of papal Rome." Later in the article we find: "We became Christian through Rome, but through Byzantium we became merely Orthodox" (Vasile Hanu, "Blajul şi românismul integral," *Unirea* 8, no. 8 [August 1997]: 5).

44. I use this word to mean the more heavily nationalist Orthodox, whose position resembles that of the "Orthodoxists" or "Gândirists" of the 1930s. Through the writings of such thinkers as Nichifor Crainic, Simion

Mehedinți, and Nae Ionescu, those years saw extensive elaboration of a national ideology linking Romanian national character organically with Orthodoxy. (That view fails to account for how Orthodoxy created Romanianness when the same religion also included various "Slavs.")

45. See, e.g., Ioan Moisin, "Situația Bisericii Române Unite în primele opt luni din actuala guvernare," *Viața creștină* 8 no. 16 (August 1997): 3.

46. See Andrei Mureșanu, "Cît de catolici au fost corifeii 'Școlii Ardelene'?" *Vatra* 1(1998):81–83; Gabriel Andreescu, "Mesajul ÎPS Bartolomeu Anania," *22* 9, no. 14 (7–13 April 1998): 4.

47. Again, in a less conflict-ridden moment, the argument for his national heroism could have become grounds for a reconciliation between the two churches—indeed, that was the hope of at least some who became involved in the plan. A Greek Catholic monk told me that the Vatican's papal nuncio in Romania had raised the possibility of returning Inochentie as a way of initiating a reconciliation; I heard the same view from several Orthodox also, and it appeared in one of the newspaper reports after Inochentie's reburial.

48. Although one of Romanians' most attractive characteristics is their capacity for strong feeling, it has only rarely happened to me as an interviewer that people I scarcely know weep during our discussion.

49. Verdery 1996: chapter 3, pp. 74–79; chapter 4, pp. 92–97. Cf. Borneman 1992.

50. Think, for example, of Michael the Brave, Tudor Vladimirescu, and the peasant rebel Horea. Others, such as princes Stephen the Great and Vlad Țepeș, suffered merely the ignominy of holding back the Turkish invasion for an ungrateful Christendom, or they died tragically young (Mihai Eminescu), or mad (Avram Iancu), or far away (Nicolae Bălcescu).

51. Over my quarter-century of research in Romania I have seen countless times how *personally* Romanians of all stripes still feel the West's betrayal of them at Yalta, and again (they believe) at Malta. Many also feel the reluctance of Western investors to flood Romania with funds and aid after 1989 as a kind of betrayal: "You promised us that if we threw off communism you would help us, and now you're doing nothing."

52. Orthodoxy perceives a material threat from Greek Catholics not only with respect to church buildings but beyond this, for Greek Catholics offer competition in the strict market sense: they're cheaper. I do not want to imply that possible believers *make* this calculation in joining a church, but the material aspect bears mention. For centuries, Orthodox priests have lined

their pockets with fees charged for various services: baptisms, weddings, and funerals, of course, but a host of others, too, such as annual blessing of the threshold, periodic remembrances of the dead, sanctifying crops or boundaries, and so on. Acquiring the materials for these remembrances (such as food, candles, wine, etc.) can be fairly costly by local standards, as I discovered when I requested one such service for my recently departed brother. Greek Catholics find fewer such services to be necessary, and they charge less for them.

The "economizing" argument also favors fundamentalist Protestants, who are cheaper still (one should not forget their lavish funding from abroad) and whose faithful are not expected to spend huge sums on life-cycle rituals, as do Orthodox and Catholics. Fundamentalist Protestants also offer very valuable services not available from the Orthodox Church, such as assistance with problems of daily living, as well as a social message suited to confusing times. According to two Baptist missionaries with whom I spoke, their emphasis is on "correcting doctrinal errors" propagated by the Orthodox Church, which, as they see it, is not evangelical and does not adequately emphasize the teachings of the Bible. Therefore, Baptists hope to win converts though Bible study, leading to religious adherence based on belief rather than on "tradition," as is the Orthodox emphasis.

53. The Protestants most active in the religious "market" are not entirely the same as those involved in property conflicts and in the Transylvanian history I summarized earlier. The former are chiefly fundamentalist Protestants, mostly from the United States, whereas the latter are primarily Lutherans, Calvinists, and Unitarians. According to the 1992 Romanian census, here are the percentages of the total population for some of these faiths: Orthodox (86.8 percent), Roman Catholic (5.0), Calvinist (3.5), Greek Catholic (1.0), Pentecostals/ Adventists/Baptists (1.8), Lutherans (0.2).

54. Here is an Orthodox monk who thinks that faith runs if not in the blood, at least in the mother's milk: "Hold to the faith that you sucked from your mothers' breasts!" (Cleopa 1997:88). That faith is inherited is an argument I heard even from an urban intellectual in Cluj, an Orthodox who found herself attracted to Greek Catholicism. Nonetheless, she had decided not to convert, she said, on these grounds: "If my ancestors hadn't been Orthodox, I'd switch. But since my forebears in the eighteenth century fought so hard against becoming Greek Catholics, for me to switch now would be a betrayal! One must be consistent."

55. Andrei Mureşanu, "Cît de catolici au fost corifeii 'Şcolii Ardelene'?" *Vatra* 1 (1998): 81–83

56. Following Romania's 1996 elections, this often occurred with the active support of Romania's president, Emil Constantinescu. In part to emphasize his difference from the previous government of Iliescu (whose past as a high-level apparatchik prevented his wholehearted embrace of Orthodoxy after 1989), as of 1996 Constantinescu appeared frequently in public with Romanian Patriarch Teoctist at his side. Aside from this alliance, which may have been at Constantinescu's initiative, the Orthodox Church has taken its own steps to ensure its position.

57. I do not know the politicking behind this outcome, but I imagine it had something to do with the inevitable objections of non-Orthodox national minorities, particularly Hungarians.

58. Archbishop Daniel of Moldova, "Prozelitism şi democraţie," *Scara* 1, no. 2 (1997): 22–23.

59. Cleopa 1997:87–88.

60. *Current Digest of the Post-Soviet Press* 49, no. 30 (1997): 10. As an aside: National Public Radio's *Morning Edition* for 30 September 1997 reported that Mormons were very upset with the new law, which would seriously disrupt their missionary efforts in Russia. They protested their exclusion from the first tier (religions recognized fifteen years previously), arguing that because they were in Russia before the 1917 Revolution, they qualify under the new "age" restriction.

61. Michael R. Gordon, "Russians Pass Bill Sharply Favoring Orthodox Church," *New York Times*, 20 September 1997, pp. 1, 5.

62. Ibid. Some Russians also saw the proposed law in these terms. For example, an article in the Russian paper *Sevodnya* in July 1997 stated: "The Church is behaving like certain 'domestic goods producers' that are seeking to protect themselves from their more vigorous foreign competitors with high tariffs. In that sense, the basic competition is perhaps between the Russian Orthodox Church and . . . the Vatican. . . . Meanwhile, many Russian citizens have sought answers to difficult problems of their lives in the period of 'buccaneer capitalism' not at all from Orthodox priests . . . [but from] Aum Shinrikyo and the Rev. Moon" (*Current Digest of the Post-Soviet Press* 49 no. 30 [1997]: 11).

63. *Moscow News* in 1997 published an article entitled "Religious Programs Strike Out with Russian TV Viewers" that cast further light on the problems of Orthodoxy. It reported that the audience for the religious programs of the Orthodox Television Agency, a "supermonopoly on religious

programming," stood at a dismal 1 percent of TV viewers (*Moscow News*, 29 May–3 June 1997, p. 12).

64. Orthodox Archbishop Chrysostom of Vilnius and Lithuania, for example, put the problem thus: "[T]oday a lot of young clergy blame my generation for staining the purity of Orthodoxy and bringing the Russian Orthodox Church into danger of joining the heretics—above all the Catholics—by searching for unity" (*Moscow News*, 24–30 July 1997, p. 10). In late January 1998, Orthodox Church states held a meeting at which they made anti-Western and anti-NATO declarations. Those represented were Russia, Ukraine, Belarus, Armenia, Bulgaria, and Georgia (*RFE/RL Newsline* 2, no. 15 [23 January 1998].

65. These include a speech he delivered at Georgetown University that was widely (and perhaps wrongly) interpreted as obstructing the possibility of reconciliation (*Newsweek*, 3 November 1997, p. 64). In addition, he canceled his attendance at the June 1997 meeting in Graz and neglected to send the customary delegation to an annual festivity at the Vatican. My thanks to Rev. Mr. Ronald Robertson for clarifying this question.

66. At the insistence of several Orthodox churches, the status of Greek or Byzantine Catholicism in relation to Orthodox countries was raised at the sixth plenary meeting of the Joint International Commission for Theological Dialogue Between the Roman Catholic Church and the Orthodox Church (Friesing, Germany, June 1990). An official joint statement of a provisional nature emerged from these discussions; three years later, at the seventh plenary meeting in Lebanon, it was revised and published as the Balamand Document. In 1992, the Vatican had issued a further document, *Pro Russia*, in response to concerns expressed by Orthodox churches as to the place of Greek Catholicism in the Vatican's policies toward Orthodoxy (see Roberson 1995). The entire series was aimed at allaying Orthodox fears about Roman Catholic proselytizing in their countries, but those fears appear still to be active. My thanks to Rev. Mr. Ronald Roberson for a discussion that clarified these matters for me.

67. For example, in mid-January 1998, Russian Orthodox and Roman Catholic officials sent a delegation to Ukraine to resolve a dispute over church buildings. The Russian Orthodox Church argued that Greek Catholics had unlawfully taken church buildings in western Ukraine (*RFE/RL Newsline* 2, no. 10, [16 January 1998]). On the whole, however, these disputes are far less contentious than in Romania, for Ukrainian Greek Catholics received back most of the church buildings they need.

68. *New York Times*, 12 June 1997, p. A15. According to Rev. Mr. Ronald

Roberson, the decision was not Patriarch Alexei's alone: in a session of the
Holy Synod of the Russian Orthodox Church, a bloc of bishops opposed
the meeting with Pope John Paul II (Roberson, personal communication).

69. I have been unable to confirm this report but find it both plausible and likely.

70. The politics of the Orthodox–Greek Catholic dispute are even more complex than I have indicated, and they far exceed both the return of Inochentie
to Transylvania and the market metaphor that has driven my discussion.
Underlying Moscow's conflict with the Vatican, I believe, are divisions
within Russian Orthodoxy similar to those I described for Romania.
Patriarch Alexei, like Romania's Teoctist, walks a tightrope between traditionalist and modernizing clergy, all struggling fiercely to shape the direction
(and the use of resources) of the newly empowered colossus that is Russian
Orthodoxy (see *Current Digest of the Post-Soviet Press* 49, no. 30 [1997]: 11).
The maneuvering draws church leaders into the wider field of Russian politics, in which strange bedfellows are made. We see just how strange when
we learn that the chief architects of Russia's Law on Religions, establishing
an Orthodox Church monopoly, were from the Russian Communist Party
(ibid., pp. 9–10). This same report discusses the generally pro-communist
stance of Orthodox priests and the nationalist–communist alliance that
draws the two organizations together. Patriarch Alexei and the Communist
Party thus find themselves allied against Boris Yeltsin, whom they view as
kowtowing to "foreign bosses" and compromising the national values the
Orthodox Church considers itself to personify.

71. This information concerning new buildings in Cluj is from a woman active
in Greek Catholic affairs in that city.

72. The pope has stated that he will not accept the government's invitation
without a separate invitation from Romania's patriarch; that has not been
extended.

73. I have this information from a Greek Catholic monk in Cluj. My inter-
locutor's explanation as to why the pope had done this was, "He probably
didn't know what he signed—the Hungarians in the Vatican probably set
it in motion." (Hungarians are the most numerous Roman Catholics in
Romania, and most of them live in Transylvania.)

74. Since this person was among the principal actors in the plan, his view is
important to note.

75. The actual date was 19 October 1997.

76. This was the view of one woman present, who told me others had reported
the same sensation.

77. I have this report from a lapsed Orthodox friend who attended both the symposium and the reburial.

78. Note that he was of low rank; no one of the status of bishop or higher from the Orthodox Church attended the ceremony. (Perhaps they were not invited?)

79. *România liberă*, 21 October 1997, p. 11; and *Evenimentul zilei*, 20 October 1997, p. 5. Two laypeople I spoke with, one Greek Catholic and one Orthodox, expressed dismay that President Constantinescu did not attend the event, for that would have furthered the possibilities for reconciliation. (His frequent appearances with Orthodox clerics doubtless precluded his attendance.)

80. Two of the three major daily newspapers (*Adevărul, Evenimentul zilei*, and *România liberă*) carried brief reports. The last of them presented two articles (it is the paper closest to the political party in which Greek Catholics are strongest, the National Peasant Party). A brief segment of the service was carried on the evening news of Romania's national TV channel, but otherwise only special religious programs and publications gave it much space. (Thanks to Prof. Mihai Bărbulescu and Sidonia Puiu of Cluj for this information.)

81. A Greek Catholic respondent in Cluj expressed the opinion three months after the reburial that relations with the Orthodox had worsened. Even in areas where Orthodox congregations had worked out with Greek Catholics an alternating use of church buildings, she said, they were now refusing Greek Catholics access.

82. There is even some talk of proposing him for sainthood, on the grounds of his contribution to raising up the Romanian nation (the Orthodox Church has done precisely that for some other national heroes who were Orthodox).

83. The same is true of the skull of St. Andrew, as well as of several other religious figures being rediscovered, discussed, brought back, proposed for canonization, etc. They include Prince Constantin Brâncoveanu, Prince Stephen the Great, the monk Sofronie, and four ancient skeletons found in Dobrogea and subsequently canonized ("the saints of Niculițel"). A more recent saint, Ion Iacob Noul Hozevit, born in 1913, went to Jordan as an ascetic and died there in 1960; upon his exhumation seven years later, he was found not to have putrefied. Romanians found out about it only after 1989, canonized him (1992), and began efforts to bring him back to Romania (information courtesy of Rev. Mr. Doru Pușcașu).

84. Ion Zubaşcu, "Osemintele episcopului Ioan Inochenţiu Micu Klein au fost înhumate în catedrala din Blaj," *România liberă*, 21 October 1997; p. 11. See also "Ioan Inochenţiu Micu-Klein s-a întors acasă," *Viaţa creştină* 8, no. 16 (August 1997): 3.

85. This phrase was quoted from Inochentie's correspondence in exile, on the occasion of his final return to Blaj on 3, August 1997 (*Viaţa creştină* 8, no. 16 [August 1997]: 4).

3. GIVING PROPER BURIAL, RECONFIGURING SPACE AND TIME

1. Thanks to Pamela Ballinger both for urging me to include this material and for helping me to do so. Her further contributions to the chapter are evident throughout the notes.

2. Herein lies the difference between Yugoslavia and the other two collapsed federal states, Czechoslovakia and the Soviet Union: with the exception of Chechnya and the Caucasus, violence did not accompany the creation of new states from the former federations.

3. See, e.g., Verdery 1996: chapter 4; Slezkine 1994; Vujačić and Zaslavsky 1991.

4. See Ballinger 1998:241–242.

5. I mentioned there the reburial of Vlatko Maček and the concomitant plans to rebury Ante Pavelić (not realized). Another person reburied was conservative Serbian theologian Nikolaj Velimirovic, who died in exile in the United States and was reinterred in Serbia with much pomp in the early 1990s. Information courtesy of Wendy Bracewell, Cambridge University.

6. In Emir Kusturica's film *Underground* we see the connection of the two kinds of corpses neatly compressed in the figure of Ivan, who died in World War II but comes back to life in the present wars and avenges himself by killing his brother Marko. (Marko's last words are "A war isn't a war until a brother kills a brother.")

7. Cited in Gligorov 1995:511.

8. Ballinger 1998; Denich 1994; Hayden 1994. My discussion below draws liberally on these three texts.

9. See Denitch 1994:30–31.

10. Djilas 1977:447.

11. Denich 1994:370.

12. Denich 1994.

13. Ballinger 1998: chapter 6.

14. Hayden 1994:179.

15. Thanks to Gail Kligman for this thought.

16. Thanks to Dr. Ljiljana Smajlović and Goranka Matić for obtaining this photograph for me, from the photo documentation archive of the Belgrade publication *Vreme*.

17. For example, a 1997 report discussed the nearly two thousand bodies that had been exhumed from thirty-one mass graves and hundreds of smaller ones scattered across Bosnia (OMRI News, 6 February 1997).

18. These uses of bones were not new to Yugoslav politics. As already mentioned, Prince Lazar's travels arose from bone symbolism relating to monarchs and saints. Moreover, Renata Salecl reports:

> The national conflict between the Serbs and the Albanians, as well as that between Serbs and Macedonians has always used the symbolism of stealing bones from Serbian graves. A mythology has even been created by which Albanians are [thought] to dig up the graves of Serbian children, and Macedonians . . . to have used the bones of Serbian soldiers who fell in the First World War for anatomical studies in their medical faculties. (Salecl 1996:421)

19. Thanks to Susan Woodward for the view contained in this and the following paragraph, and for a highly informative discussion of the problem of dead bodies in Yugoslavia.

20. See the excellent discussion in Woodward 1995: chapter 8, esp. pp. 236–246.

21. Bosnians can also be Orthodox Serbs or Catholic Croats, since the Republic of Bosnia-Herzegovina contained people of all three religions and nationalities.

22. The pope may also have calculated that as Islam, Catholicism, and Orthodoxy converged in Bosnia, Croatia, and Serbia, his greater rival was Orthodoxy; an alliance with Islamic states helped him to undermine the recalcitrant Russian Patriarch Alexei. (Recall my discussion in chapter 2.)

23. Information courtesy of Eva Huseby-Darvas, University of Michigan (Dearborn), and Ioan Cuceu, Institute of Ethnography, Cluj, Romania. See also Strathern 1992:126.

24. Hence the expression common to several languages in the region, "May the earth lie lightly upon him/her" (in Romanian, *fie-i ţărîna uşoară*; in Serbo-Croatian, *neka mu je laka zemlja*).

25. See, e.g., Douglass 1969; Christian 1972. Ballinger's 1990s ethnography among Italian exiles from Istria finds many of these same practices active in people's lives and recollections.

26. I might note that Fustel's aim in discussing the kinship–land connection

was to argue that private property is the "natural" form of property relation and has been so since ancient times. See Grossi 1981.

27. Thinking of nationalisms as ancestor cults concerned with the place of their
    dead in both space (territory) and time (genealogies) enables me to link
    nation-state creation with dead-body politics in a more emotion-laden way
    than I have so far: through the sociality of corpses as ancestors, kin, and
    spouses mourned by those who loved them and who want to see them treated
    properly. When mass graves are opened and mass funerals are held, some of
    their emotional impact as nation-building events comes from ideas about the
    fate of souls at death and their subsequent relations with the living. (To us,
    this argument obviously makes most sense for reburials of persons who died
    within living memory, although we should note that for Serbs, "living mem-
    ory" seems to mean as much as six hundred years.) See also Young 1997,
    who writes (p. 14): "Academics have accepted language that justifies killing
    of today's living with reference to past dead. . . . [This response] may seem
    more rational than an explanation [in terms of] suffering and metaphysical
    relation with the dead, but both are part of the nexus expressing concern that
    the dead did not 'die in vain.' "

28. I use the masculine pronoun because of the patrilineal bias of nationalism,
    noted in chapter 1. Although some of the nameless post-Yugoslav dead are
    doubtless female, they have not been celebrated as heroines of their nations.
    To the contrary: because of wartime rapes, they have come to symbolize the
    nation's degradation and shame.

29. Halpern, for example, writes: "The current fighting in Bosnia . . . can be
    seen as marauding lineages in modern dress—a pattern shared by not only
    orthodox Serbs and Montenegrins, but by Hercegovinian Croats and some
    Moslems" (Halpern 1994:124). He goes on to ask what external conditions
    favored the retention of kin-based social structures. He might also have
    asked under what conditions these social structures were reinforced or
    even "reinvented."

30. Thanks to Pamela Ballinger for clarifying this point.

31. Since the 1974 administrative revision of Yugoslavia, Kosovo has been a
    province subordinated within the (Federal) Republic of Serbia, as opposed
    to a fully autonomous republic, even though Serbs form a tiny minority (10
    percent) within Kosovo. The rest are Albanians.

32. Silber and Little 1995:38.

33. Thanks to Robert Hayden for this reference.

34. Stoker mixed together folk beliefs found in the late nineteenth century in

3. GIVING PROPER BURIAL

different parts of East-Central Europe.

35. According to Arkhipov (personal communication), a vampire's coffin is
    his house. It's no surprise that a vampire carries soil with him because soil
    is where he lives, as a person supposedly dead and buried; for him, soil is
    also the sine qua non of daytime travel, so Dracula *must* take his soil to
    England. Stephen Arata's reading of the novel, upon which I draw in this
    paragraph, nonetheless plausibly links this theme with the matter of
    national soils (Arata 1996).

36. McNally and Florescu 1972:148.

37. Tumarkin 1994:127.

38. Lampland writes, "The campaign for augmenting Kossuth's grave with
    historic soils [reinforced the widespread image of his] body and soul
    becoming one with the nation's soil, and so one with the nation." (It is
    unclear from Lampland's account whether this plan was in fact realized.)
    She continues: "Kossuth is represented as the soul, the spirit of the nation.
    [His] body is portrayed as the body of the nation. His death and resur-
    rection [are] the death and birth, the very apotheosis of the nation"
    (1993:33–34).

39. From the immense literature on this topic, I will single out for illustration
    Khyrghyz writer Chingiz Aitmatov's novel *The Day Lasts More Than a
    Hundred Years*—a marvelous book unified by the problem of giving some-
    one a proper burial despite the obstacles posed by a modernizing Soviet soci-
    ety. Strewn throughout it are the hero Yedigei's thoughts about how to treat
    his dead friend's corpse. For instance, as he strives to remember the words of
    the prayer for the dead that will bring reconciliation and calm, he thinks,
    "You [don't] simply shout at God, 'Why have you arranged things so that
    people are born and die?' . . . These prayers have been unchanged since [the
    world began]. . . . These words, polished over thousands of years like bars
    of gold, were the last a living man had to say over a dead man. That was the
    custom." And as he realizes that none of the younger men present knows the
    prayers, he asks himself, "How then could they bury one another?" (p. 97).
    Yedigei is contrasted with another character who, captured and tortured, has
    lost all memory of his kin, living and dead, and of his own identity. He serves
    in the novel as a reminder that without our place in a line of ancestors and
    heirs, without acknowledging our dead, we are not human.

40. See Ballinger 1998; Barber 1988; Bringa 1995; Eliade 1955, 1970; Halpern
    and Halpern 1972; Kligman 1988 (her data come from both Greek Catholic
    and Orthodox informants); McNally and Florescu 1972; and Young 1997.

I should note that within any given group, there may be both diverse beliefs and practices about burial and different levels of commitment to them. This makes it difficult to contrast something like "Serb" mortuary practices, for instance, with "Croat" ones, or "Christian" with "Muslim" ones, for the internal variety can be as great as the comparative differences. At most, we can say that such beliefs and practices are worth looking into—for post-Yugoslav cases as well as others—and that even the modern urbanite may feel their effects, however tenuously (like the Moscow intellectuals who want to see Lenin properly buried).

41. According to the Halperns, a proper burial in certain areas of Serbia (like burials elsewhere in Southeastern Europe) involves careful completion of certain rituals: throwing coins into the coffin to help the soul on its journey, giving it messages to take to other dead souls, having the corpse ask forgiveness of the survivors, making a large feast to be eaten next to the grave so the dead can partake of it, following up with feasts on specific dates after the death, and so on (Halpern and Halpern 1972:108). When people are thrown into caves or mass grave sites without these rituals, local practice in some places would put a black dog nearby to keep the victims from escaping to torment their killers (Ballinger 1998:187).

42. Djilas 1977:149.

43. Ballinger 1998. This kind of behavior is not, of course, limited to Serbia but is found worldwide. Specifically for Eastern Europe, after 1989 numerous Jewish cemeteries and tombstones were vandalized.

44. Stephen Kinzer, "Ousted Croats Go to Seized Towns," *New York Times*, 28 October 1992, p. A9. Thanks to Pamela Ballinger for this reference.

   Barber comments that in a Szekler area of Transylvania, villagers used to fire rifles into the grave to prevent the dead person from returning to disturb them (Barber 1988:54). In that case, however, the graves were not of enemies.

45. Hertz 1960. Cf. Huntington and Metcalf 1979.

46. Thanks to Ashraf Ghani for this idea. See also Rév 1995:30.

47. Bringa 1995.

48. Information in this paragraph is courtesy of Susan Woodward.

49. This is not strictly a "Slavic" practice, for it also appears in Pamela Ballinger's work on the Italian exodus from the Istrian peninsula after World War II. She found a letter from 1946 in which Italian officials wrote:

   The rumours are that the cemeteries of Italian prisoners dead in Jugoslavia are being destroyed. The population which has already seen the tombstones of the Italian martyrs lifted did not wish to leave even their dead to Jugoslavia. Several people are already taking steps to have their dead exhumed. Would you therefore approach the Trieste authorities to find a way of transferring bodies to Trieste. (Ballinger 1998:119)

In addition, she writes of the exhumation of hero Nazario Sauro, whom the exiles refused to leave for the "barbarian" Slavs to dishonor; they took him to Italy instead.

50. Information courtesy of a report from Dražen Prelec, Sloan Management School.
51. Ballinger 1998:199, 237–246.
52. From Wendy Bracewell's work on transhumant Vlachs in Albania, we learn that they have no idea where their ancestors are buried (Bracewell, personal communication). This apparently goes with not seeing bounded territory as vital to identity—an idea that would definitely put a damper on exhumatory politics.
53. See also Povrzanović 1997:2, 6.
54. Anthropologist Jane Schneider organized a panel around this theme at the 1997 Annual Meeting of the American Anthropological Association, Washington, D.C. The papers presented covered Latin America, Europe, Southeast Asia, and the Middle East, under the title "Retributive Justice and Regime Changes: Toward Democratic Accountability or an International Property Regime?"
55. See Borneman 1997.
56. Lustration laws sought to prevent people who had held positions of responsibility in the communist period from doing so again after 1989. Enforcing lustration proved complicated, since aside from the most visible party leaders, it was not clear how far down the scale of "collaborators" one should or could go. The complexities were dramatized in the famed case of Jan Caval, whose claims to being a dissident in exile were challenged when Czech Secret Police files indicated that he had been an informer (he denied the charge), thus nullifying his election to the Czech Parliament.
57. Ballinger 1998: chapter 6.
58. If it has proved almost impossible to compel Serbs and Croats to turn over their war criminals, perhaps the reason is that the two kinds of social actors constituted by the Serbs and Croats and by the Hague are effectively incompatible, as are the kinds of enforceable punishment suited to each.

Bogdan Denitch suggests one possible implication of the difference when he writes, "Democracy requires that people be responsible for their own personal guilt, not that of their family, tribe, or nationality," and he rails against the stupidity that holds *all* Serbs or *all* Croats responsible for killings (Denitch 1994:33).

59. For example, Cohen and Odhiambo 1992; Dennie 1996; Gal 1989, and 1991; Lampland 1993; Rév 1995.

60. It is not only in the postsocialist world that this is occurring: Western authors have also been writing out the communist period (e.g., Robert Kaplan's *Balkan Ghosts*). Thanks to Pamela Ballinger for this observation.

61. Stunning evidence of this practice is found in King 1997 and Khaldei 1997. The falsification of history and the theme of airbrushing lie at the heart of Milan Kundera's *The Book of Laughter and Forgetting*.

62. Rév 1995:25.

63. Tropes of resurrection abound in postsocialist societies, and parades of dead bodies signify this beautifully. Handling the dead does more than simply indicate the death of communism and the resurrection of older continuities, however: it also creates communities of mourners, of "family" for these "ancestors," of those who will be present at the resurrection and included among the "saved," and those who will be ejected into damnation.

64. My thanks to Lynn Hunt for this point.

65. Recall the attempt by the Hungarian furnace tycoon to gain acceptance for bones putatively of Petőfi but, according to experts, actually those of a young Jewish girl (see the introduction), as well as the possibility that Inochentie Micu's bones may well have arrived in Transylvania together with those of other clerics buried near his sarcophagus (chapter 2). Thanks to Jeremy King for reminding me of this point.

66. Judah 1997:135–136.

67. *New York Times*, 2 December 1997, p. A4. Messages sent to Tito's home page (http://www.fer.uni-lj.si/tito) include the following: "While you were here we had a life. When you died the idiots took over, and the world has seen the result. I send you this message from Sweden." Tito sometimes answers ("To all who want me back. I am not crazy. Tito"). Or, failing this, one can click on an icon that produces his best speeches.

68. A further sign that something cosmic is going on, something involving mortality, time, heroes, nations, ancestors, etc., is that along with the concern about graves and reburials there is an equivalent preoccupation with resurrection, rebirth, and birth itself. I cannot enter into this vast subject, other than to say that throughout Eastern Europe (and especially

in former Yugoslavia), not only are metaphors of rebirth rampant but so is an active politics of reproduction. In nearly every country of the region, pro-natalist nationalists have been pushing for an end to abortion, which (unlike other forms of contraception) was readily available in socialist times. The redefinition of nations and regimes since 1989 thus brings with it concern for national resurrection/rebirth and for a high birthrate to exhibit the nation's health. This is especially true in former Yugoslavia. (See, inter alia, Kligman 1996; Supek 1991; Verdery 1996: chapter 3.) Birth, death, and resurrection are indeed "cosmic" matters, and they have informed much postsocialist politicking throughout the 1990s.

69. For example, groups and individuals differ in whether they experience rewriting history or revising genealogies as a cosmological reordering. I suspect that is more likely when the bones and corpses being handled take on an air of sanctity, becoming somehow part of the revival of religion after years of official atheism. This thought might explain the widespread public interest aroused by the peregrinations of Prince Lazar in Serbia, for instance.

70. Rév 1995:32.

71. Let me illustrate this with an extract from an article by a Romanian writer celebrating election day in November 1996, when the old-apparatchik regime of Ion Iliescu fell from power.

> [This] day will become Romania's rational rather than national holiday, through our country's return to continuity with its prior history and to the normality of Europe's open horizons. . . . Fifty years ago, local communists, supported by the Soviet army and the tacit complicity of the West, snatched Romania from its normal history. . . . What happened in the communist period in Russia and the other sovietized countries was an aberrant experiment contrary to these societies' sense of purpose; they were torn as if by a crashing meteorite from their [normal] national and European continuities. . . . [On this day] then, Romanians recover their historical rationality. . . . [We revalorize] the history of our patriotic and diligent princes, of our free middle peasantry and our previous political parties, of the constitutional monarchy. . . . [and] of a social-democratic bourgeoisie. (Hurezeanu 1996:1)

72. See Verdery 1996: chapter 2; Binns 1979–1980.

73. See Hammel 1968.

74. I am grateful to Ashraf Ghani for this point, and for a stimulating conversation on the question of ancestors and temporality.

75. Thanks to Caroline Humphrey, Cambridge University, for suggesting this point.

76. My thanks to G. W. Skinner for an illuminating discussion of the shapes of history and kinship.

77. Leach 1961:114–136. He goes on to posit a third kind, time that is thought to oscillate.

78. Cf. Bourdieu 1977; Zerubavel 1981.

79. In the example he discusses, the bearers of a cyclical temporality see agency as coming from outside themselves, such as from ghosts or dead ancestors, as against the Chinese Communist Party's progressive linear "socialist road" that was to be constructed by human agents acting deliberately. See Mueggler 1999.

80. See, e.g., Lovell 1992; Mueggler 1999.

81. See Verdery 1996: chapter 2.

82. I personally have heard this view (along with a certain nostalgia for the relaxed old days of socialism) from Romanians, Hungarians, Czechs, Poles, Ukrainians, and Russians.

83. My thanks to Jeremy King for this point and the illustrative example.

84. See Harvey 1989; Verdery 1996: chapter 1.

85. See Harvey 1989.

REFERENCES

Abrahamian, Levon Hm. 1997. "Mythology of Soviet and Post-Soviet Leaders: I. Lenin as Trickster." Unpublished MS.

Aitmatov, Chingiz. 1988. *The Day Lasts More Than a Hundred Years.* Bloomington: Indiana University Press.

Albu, Corneliu. 1983. *Pe urmele lui Ion-Inocenţiu Micu-Klein.* Bucharest: Editura Sport-Turism.

Anderson, Benedict. 1983. *Imagined Communities: Reflections on the Origin and Spread of Nationalism.* London: Verso.

Andreesco, Anca, and Ioana Bacou. 1986. *Mourir dans les Carpathes.* Paris: Payot.

Andrusz, Gregory, Michael Harloe, and Ivan Szelenyi, eds. 1996. *Cities After Socialism: Urban and Regional Change and Conflict in Post-Socialist Societies.* Oxford: Blackwell.

Arata, Stephen D. 1996. "The Occidental Tourist: Stoker and Reverse

Colonization." In *Fictions of Loss in the Victorian Fin de Siècle*. Cambridge: Cambridge University Press.

Ballinger, Pamela. 1998. "Submerged Politics, Exiled Histories: Memory and Identity at the Borders of the Balkans." Ph.D. diss., Johns Hopkins University.

Barber, Paul. 1988. *Vampires, Burial, and Death: Folklore and Reality*. New Haven: Yale University Press.

Barraud, Cécile, Daniel de Coppet, André Iteanu, and Raymond Jamous. 1994. *Of Relations and the Dead: Four Societies Viewed from the Angle of Their Exchanges*. Oxford: Berg.

Benjamin, Walter. 1969. *Illuminations*. New York: Schocken.

Berdiaev, Nicolas. 1937. *The Origin of Russian Communism*. New York: Charles Scribner.

Binns, C. A. P. 1979–1980. "The Changing Face of Power: Revolution and Accommodation in the Development of the Soviet Ceremonial System." *Man* 14:585–606, 15:170–187.

Bloch, Maurice, and Jonathan Parry. 1982. *Death and the Regeneration of Life*. Cambridge: Cambridge University Press.

Bonnell, Victoria A. 1997. *The Iconography of Power: Soviet Political Posters Under Lenin and Stalin*. Berkeley: University of California Press.

Borneman, John. 1992. *Belonging in the Two Berlins: Kin, State, Nation*. Cambridge: Cambridge University Press.

——. 1997. *Settling Accounts: Violence, Justice, and Accountability in Postsocialist Europe*. Princeton: Princeton University Press.

Bourdieu, Pierre. 1977. *Outline of a Theory of Practice*. Cambridge: Cambridge University Press.

Bringa, Tone. 1995. *Being Muslim the Bosnian Way: Identity and Community in a Central Bosnian Village*. Princeton: Princeton University Press.

Brown, Peter. 1981. *The Cult of the Saints: Its Rise and Function in Late Christianity*. Chicago: University of Chicago Press.

Bruszt, László, and David Stark. 1992. "Remaking the Political Field in Hungary: From the Politics of Confrontation to the Politics of Competition." In *Eastern Europe in Revolution*, Ivo Banac, ed., pp. 13–55. Ithaca, N.Y.: Cornell University Press.

Butler, Judith. 1990. *Gender Trouble: Feminism and the Subversion of Identity*. New York: Routledge.

——. 1993. *Bodies That Matter: On the Discursive Limits of "Sex."* New York: Routledge.

Bynum, Caroline Walker. 1995a. *The Resurrection of the Body in Western Christianity, 200–1336.* New York: Columbia University Press.

———. 1995b. "Why All the Fuss About the Body? A Medievalist's Perspective." *Critical Inquiry* 22:1–33.

Campeanu, Pavel. 1994. *Romania: Coada pentru hrană, un mod de viață.* Bucharest: Editura Litera.

Christian, William. 1972. *Person and God in a Spanish Valley.* New York: Seminar Press.

Cipăianu, George. 1997. "Une Église 'réduite au silence': Les Gréco-Catholiques roumains et le comunisme." *Transylvanian Review* 6:71–82.

Cleopa, Ilie (Arhimandrite). 1997. "In dreaptă credinţă a neamului românesc." *Scara* 1, no. 2:87–88.

Cohen, David William, and E. S. Atieno Odhiambo. 1992. *Burying SM: The Politics of Knowledge and the Sociology of Power in Africa.* Portsmouth, NH: Heinemann; London: James Curry.

Comaroff, Jean, and John Comaroff. 1998. "Occult Economies and the Violence of Abstraction: Notes from the South African Postcolony." *American Ethnologist* 26 (forthcoming).

Connell, R. W. 1987. *Gender and Power: Society, the Person and Sexual Politics.* Stanford: Stanford University Press.

———. 1990. "The State, Gender, and Sexual Politics." *Theory and Society* 19:507–544.

Creed, Gerald. 1995. "The Politics of Agriculture in Bulgaria." *Slavic Review* 54:843–868.

Danforth, Loring, and Alexander Tsiaras. 1982. *The Death Rituals of Rural Greece.* Princeton: Princeton University Press.

Delaney, Carol. 1994. "Father State, Motherland, and the Birth of Modern Turkey." In *Naturalizing Power: Essays in Feminist Cultural Analysis,* Sylvia Yanagisako and Carol Delaney, eds., pp. 177–199. New York and London: Routledge.

Denich, Bette. 1994. "Dismembering Yugoslavia: Nationalist Ideologies and the Symbolic Revival of Genocide." *American Ethnologist* 21:367–390.

Denitch, Bogdan. 1994. *Ethnic Nationalism: The Tragic Death of Yugoslavia.* Minneapolis: University of Minnesota Press.

Dennie, Garrey Michael. 1996. "The Cultural Politics of Burial in South Africa, 1884–1990." Ph.D. diss., Johns Hopkins University.

Djilas, Milovan. 1977. *Wartime.* New York and London: Harcourt Brace Jovanovich.

Douglass, William. 1969. *Death in Murelaga: Funerary Ritual in a Spanish Basque Village*. Seattle: University of Washington Press.

Dragomir, Silviu. 1920. *Istoria desrobirei religioase a românilor din Ardeal în secolul XVIII*. Vol. 1. Sibiu: Tipografia Arhidiecezană.

Durkheim, Émile. 1915. *The Elementary Forms of the Religious Life*. London: George Allen & Unwin.

Eliade, Mircea. 1955. *The Myth of the Eternal Return*. London: Routledge.

———. 1970. *Zalmoxis, The Vanishing God: Comparative Studies in the Religions and Folklore of Dacia and Eastern Europe*. Chicago: University of Chicago Press.

Elias, Norbert. 1992. *Time: An Essay*. Oxford: Blackwell.

Eloy Martínez, Tomás. 1996. *Santa Evita*. New York: Knopf.

Feeley-Harnik, Gillian. 1991. *A Green Estate: Restoring Independence in Madagascar*. Washington, D.C.: Smithsonian Institution Press.

Floca, Ioan M. 1993. *Din istoria dreptului românesc. Dreptul scris*. Vol. 1, Sibiu: POLSIB S.A.

French, R. A., and F. E. I. Hamilton, eds. 1979. *The Socialist City: Spatial Structure and Urban Policy*. Chichester, U.K.: John Wiley.

Fustel de Coulanges, Denis Numa. 1980. *The Ancient City*. Baltimore: Johns Hopkins University Press.

Gal, Susan. 1989. "Ritual and Public Discourse in Socialist Hungary: Nagy Imre's Funeral." Unpublished MS.

———. 1991. "Bartók's Funeral: Representations of Europe in Hungarian Political Rhetoric." *American Ethnologist* 18:440–458.

———. 1998. "Political Culture and the Making of Tradition: A Comment." *Austrian History Yearbook* 29:249–260.

García Márquez, Gabriel. 1995. *Of Love and Other Demons*. New York: Knopf.

Geary, Patrick. 1978. *Furta Sacra: Thefts of Relics in the Central Middle Ages*. Princeton: Princeton University Press.

Geertz, Clifford. 1980. *Negara: The Theatre State in Nineteenth-Century Bali*. Princeton: Princeton University Press.

Gligorov, Vladimir. 1995. "What If They Will Not Give Up?" *East European Politics and Societies* 9: 499–512.

Grass, Günter. 1992. *The Call of the Toad*. New York: Harcourt Brace Jovanovich.

Greenfield, Jeanette. 1989. *The Return of Cultural Treasures*. Cambridge: Cambridge University Press.

Grossi, Paolo. 1981. *An Alternative to Private Property: Collective Property in the Juridical Consciousness of the Nineteenth Century*. Chicago: University of Chicago Press.

Guber, Rosana. 1990. "Democracy Handcuffed: The Profanation of Perón's Grave." Unpublished MS.

Halpern, Joel. 1994. "Contemporary Research on the Balkan Family, Anthropological and Historical Approaches." In *Rapports du septième congrés international d'études du sud-est européen*, pp. 103–132. Athens: Association Internationale d'Études du Sud-Est Européen.

Halpern, Joel, and Barbara Kerewsky Halpern. 1972. *A Serbian Village in Historical Perspective.* New York: Holt, Rinehart and Winston.

Hammel, Eugene. 1968. *Alternative Social Structures and Ritual Relations in the Balkans.* Englewood Cliffs, N.J.: Prentice-Hall.

Hareven, Tamara K. 1982. *Family Time and Industrial Time: The Relationship Between the Family and Work in a New England Industrial Community.* Cambridge: Cambridge University Press.

Harvey, David. 1989. *The Condition of Postmodernity.* Oxford: Blackwell.

Hauser, Ewa. 1995. "Traditions of Patriotism, Questions of Gender: The Case of Poland." In *Postcommunism and the Body Politic*, Ellen E. Berry, ed., pp. 78–104. New York: New York University Press.

Hayden, Robert M. 1994. "Recounting the Dead: The Discovery and Redefinition of Wartime Massacres in Late- and Post-Communist Yugoslavia." In *Memory, History, and Opposition Under State Socialism*, Rubie S. Watson, ed., pp. 167–184. Santa Fe, N.M.: School of American Research Press.

Hertz, Robert. 1960. *Death and the Right Hand.* Glencoe, Ill.: Free Press.

Hobsbawm, Eric, and Terence Ranger, eds. 1983. *The Invention of Tradition.* Cambridge: Cambridge University Press.

Hochschild, Adam. 1994. *The Unquiet Ghost: Russians Remember Stalin.* New York: Penguin.

Humphrey, Caroline. 1996/7. "Myth-making, Narratives, and the Dispossessed in Russia." *Cambridge Anthropology* 19, no. 2: 70–92.

Huntington, Richard, and Peter Metcalf. 1979. *Celebrations of Death: The Anthropology of Mortuary Ritual.* Cambridge: Cambridge University Press.

Hurezeanu, Emil. 1996. "O sărbătoare raţională." *22* (20–26 November 1998): 1.

Joas, Hans. 1993. *Pragmatism and Social Theory.* Chicago: University of Chicago Press.

John Paul Jones: A Commemoration. 1907. Washington, D.C.: U.S. Government Printing Office.

Jowitt, Kenneth. 1987. "Moscow 'Centre.' " *Eastern European Politics and Societies* 1:296–345.

Judah, Tim. 1997. *The Serbs: History, Myth and the Destruction of Yugoslavia.* New Haven: Yale University Press.

Kaplan, Robert. 1994. *Balkan Ghosts: A Journey Through History*. New York: Vintage.

Karl, Terry Lynn. 1990. "Dilemmas of Democratization in Latin America." *Comparative Politics* 23, no. 1:1–21.

Khaldei, Yevgeny. 1997. *Eyewitness to History: The Photographs of Yevgeny Khaldei*. New York: Aperture. With a biographical essay by Alexander Nakhimovsky and Alice Nakhimovsky.

King, David. 1997. *The Commissar Vanishes: The Falsification of Photographs and Art in Stalin's Russia*. New York: Metropolitan Books.

Kligman, Gail. 1988. *The Wedding of the Dead: Ritual, Poetics, and Popular Culture in Transylvania*. Berkeley: University of California Press.

———. 1996. "Gendering Women's Identities in Postcommunist Eastern Europe." In *Identities in Transition: Russia and Eastern Europe After Communism*, Victoria Bonnell, ed., pp. 68–91. Berkeley: University of California, International and Area Studies.

Koselleck, Reinhart. 1994. "Einleitung." In *Der politische Totenkult: Kriegerdenkmäler in der Moderne*, Reinhart Koselleck and Michael Jeismann, eds., pp. 9–20. Munich: Wilhelm Fink Verlag.

Kundera, Milan. 1980. *The Book of Laughter and Forgetting*. New York: Alfred A. Knopf.

Lampland, Martha. 1993. "Death of a Hero: Hungarian National Identity and the Funeral of Lajos Kossuth." *Hungarian Studies* 8, no. 1:29–35.

Leach, E. R. 1961. *Rethinking Anthropology*. London: Athlone.

Lovell, Ann. 1992. "Seizing the Moment: Power, Contingency, and Temporality in Street Life." In *The Politics of Time*, Henry Rutz, ed., pp. 86–107. Washington, D.C.: American Ethnological Society.

McNally, Raymond, and Radu Florescu. 1972. *In Search of Dracula: A True History of Dracula and Vampire Legends*. Greenwich, Conn.: New York Graphic Society.

Morison, Samuel Eliot. 1959. *John Paul Jones: A Sailor's Biography*. Boston: Little, Brown.

Mueggler, Erik. 1999. "Spectral Subversions: Rival Tactics of Time and Agency in Southwestern China." *Comparative Studies in Society and History* 41 (forthcoming).

Munn, Nancy. 1986. *The Fame of Gawa: A Symbolic Study of Value Transformation in a Massim (Papua New Guinea) Society*. Cambridge: Cambridge University Press.

Obeyesekere, Gananath. 1990. *The Work of Culture: Symbolic Transformation in*

Psychoanalysis and Anthropology. Chicago: University of Chicago Press.

Oțetea, Andrei, ed. 1970. *The History of the Romanian People.* New York: Twayne.

Pall, Francisc. 1997. *I. M. Micu-Klein, 1745–1768.* 3 vols. Cluj-Napoca: Fundația Culturală Română, Centru de Studii Transilvane.

Peters, Ellis. 1977. *A Morbid Taste for Bones: A Medieval Whodunnit.* London: Macmillan.

Pippidi, Andrei. 1995. "Graves as Landmarks of National Identity." *Budapest Review of Books* 5, no. 3:102–110.

Platz, Stephanie. 1997. "The Transformation of Power and the Powers of Transformation: The Karabagh Movement, the Energy Crisis, and the Emergence of UFOs in Armenia at the Dawn of Independence." Unpublished MS.

Povrzanović, Maja. 1997. "Identities in War: Embodiments of Violence and Places of Belonging." *Ethnologia Europaea* 27:1–11.

Prodan, David. 1971. *Supplex Libellus Valachorum.* Bucharest: Editura Academiei.

Pusztai, Bertalan. 1997. "Collision of Identities." *Acta Ethnographica Hungarica* 42, no. 1–2:149–163.

Remnick, David. 1996. "Hammer, Sickle, and Book." *New York Review of Books*, 23 May 1996, p. 45.

Rév, István. 1995. "Parallel Autopsies." *Representations* 49:15–39.

Ries, Nancy. 1997. *Russian Talk: Culture and Conversation During Perestroika.* Ithaca, N.Y.: Cornell University Press.

Roberson, Ronald. 1995. *The Eastern Christian Churches: A Brief Survey.* Rome: Edizioni "Orientalia Christiana."

Rosenberg, Tina. 1995. *The Haunted Land: Facing Europe's Ghosts After Communism.* New York: Random House.

Salecl, Renata. 1996. "National Identity and Socialist Moral Majority." In *Becoming National: A Reader*, Geoff Eley and Ronald Grigor Suny, eds., pp. 418–425. Oxford: Oxford University Press.

Scarry, Elaine. 1985. *The Body in Pain: The Making and Unmaking of the World.* New York: Oxford University Press.

Schneider, David. 1977. "Kinship, Nationality and Religion: Toward a Definition of Kinship." In *Symbolic Anthropology*, J. Dolgin, D. Kremnitzer, and D. Schneider, eds., pp. 63–71. New York: Columbia University Press.

Silber, Laura, and Allan Little. 1995. *Yugoslavia: Death of a Nation.* New York: Penguin.

Slezkine, Yuri. 1994. "The USSR as a Communal Apartment, or How a Socialist State Promoted Ethnic Particularism." *Slavic Review* 53, no. 2: 414–452.

Snow, David A., and Robert D. Benford. 1992. "Master Frames and Cycles of Protest." In *Frontiers in Social Movement Theory*, Aldon Morris and Carol Mueller, eds., pp. 133–155. New Haven: Yale University Press.

Snow, David A., E. Burke Rochford, Jr., Steven K. Worden, and Robert D. Benford. 1986. "Frame Alignment Processes, Micromobilization, and Movement Participation." *American Sociological Review* 51:464–481.

Stahl, Henri H. 1983. *Eseuri critice despre cultură populară românească*. Bucharest: Editura Minerva.

Stoker, Bram. 1970 [1897]. *Dracula*. New York: Dodd, Mead.

Strathern, Marilyn. 1992. *Reproducing the Future: Anthropology, Kinship and the New Reproductive Technologies*. New York: Routledge.

Supek, Olga. 1991. "The Unborn Are Also Croats." Paper presented at the 1991 Annual Meetings of the American Anthropological Association, Chicago.

Taussig, Michael. 1997. *The Magic of the State*. New York: Routledge.

Thompson, E. P. 1967. "Time, Work Discipline, and Industrial Capitalism." *Past and Present* 38:56–97.

Todorov, Vladislav. 1995. *Red Square, Black Square: Organon for Revolutionary Imagination*. Albany: State University of New York Press.

Trix, Frances. 1997. "Voices of an Albanian Village in the Post-Communist Spring." Paper presented at the Center for Russian and East European Studies, University of Michigan, Ann Arbor, 3 February.

Trouillot, Michel-Rolph. 1995. *Silencing the Past: Power and the Production of History*. Boston: Beacon.

Tumarkin, Nina. 1983. *Lenin Lives! The Lenin Cult in Soviet Russia*. Cambridge, Mass.: Harvard University Press.

——. 1994. *The Living and the Dead: The Rise and Fall of the Cult of World War II in Russia*. New York: Basic Books.

Turcuş, Şerban. 1997. "Le Saint Siège dans le discours politique roumain (1947–1953)." *Transylvanian Review* 6:135–147.

Turner, Victor. 1957. *Schism and Continuity in an African Society*. Manchester, U.K.:University of Manchester Press.

Urban, Michael, with Vyacheslav Igrunov and Sergei Mitrokhin. 1997. *The Rebirth of Politics in Russia*. Cambridge: Cambridge University Press.

Verdery, Katherine. 1996. *What Was Socialism, and What Comes Next?* Princeton: Princeton University Press.

Vujačić, Veljko, and Victor Zaslavsky. 1991. "The Causes of Disintegration in the USSR and Yugoslavia." *Telos* 88:120–140.

Williams, Brackette F. "E Pluribus White? Spirit and Nation, Suffering and Virtue, Morality and Unity in American Culture." MS in progress.

Woodward, Susan. 1995. *Balkan Tragedy: Chaos and Dissolution After the Cold War*. Washington, D.C.: Brookings Institution Press.

Yampolsky, Mikhail. 1995. "In the Shadow of Monuments." In *Soviet Hieroglyphics*, Nancy Condee, ed., pp. 93–112. Bloomington: Indiana University Press.

Young, Kathleen. 1997. "Mama Died Hungry: Reciprocal Relations Between the Living and the Dead." Unpublished MS.

Zerubavel, Eviatar. 1981. *Hidden Rhythms: Schedules and Calendars in Social Life*. Chicago: University of Chicago Press.

INDEX